THE RETURN
OF
THE DOVE

Natural Cures
They Dont Want U To Know
About

Kevin Trudeau

Front Cover Art, "Ascension" © 1993
by Kimberly Kuwica

This book is dedicated to my beloved Ana
whose eternal flame of love has kindled
the remembrance of my own.
We are forever one
in eternal life.

THE RETURN
OF THE DOVE

Empowerment to Ascension
is Written in Your Heart
Beyond the Reasoning Mind

BY
DIADRA

Wings of Spirit Foundation

Dallas, Texas U.S.A.

Published by
Wings of Spirit Foundation
6757 Arapaho, Suite 711, Box 345
Dallas, Texas 75248
(214) 233-2992

ISBN# 1-887884-00-9 (pbk.): $12.95

Printed in USA
First Edition

Cover Art: "Ascension" by Kimberly Kuwica © 1993

Copyright © 1995, Diadra Price

Edited by John A. Price

Wings of Spirit Foundation is a not-for-profit organization dedicated to the engagement of humankind in individual and collective prayer, surrendered to the Will of God [by whatever name], and to raising the consciousness of humanity to the realization of Oneness in Spirit. Through its endeavors, Wings of Spirit seeks to create an environment of harmony among all people and a world of peace.

TABLE OF CONTENTS

INTRODUCTION

INTRODUCTION

"In the beginning was the Word, and the Word was with God, and the Word was God" (John 1:1). We have come to know the "Word" as the immaculate conception in God mind of the principle of Christ Jesus made flesh in the man Jesus Christ. Such was the birth of unconditional love in the earth.

"The true light that enlightens every man was coming into the world" (John 1:9). The ministry of the Word made flesh in Jesus Christ has revealed the great truth that the way, the truth and the life of Christ indwells every human being, and no one returns to God's house except by way of this indwelling Presence.

In teaching us the way, the truth and the life, Jesus prophesied that when He went away there would be sent an inner teacher for all of us, the Holy Spirit, who would teach us all things and bring to our remembrance that which we have forgotten.

This teacher becomes fully accessible to each of us through a continuous activity of surrender and devotion to the indwelling Spirit of Truth. Communion with this teacher is inevitable as the full birth of Christ takes place in our soul.

The messages in this book were received directly from

the inner teacher, who I have come to know to be the I AM Presence of love -- the Holy Spirit. The message is presented here exactly as it was received. It has not been modified in any way. This Presence calls me Diadra, which I can only assume is the name given to my individualization of the Christ Principle. To give true authorship to that which is written in this book, I have used my spiritual name, Diadra.

This book has not come to you by chance. You can be assured it is a divinely appointed gift of the Holy Spirit sent to quicken that same Spirit in you. Each chapter contains multiple layers of meaning that will unfold with expanded awareness of Truth each time you bring yourself to its pages.

It is the prayer of my heart that, as you read this book, you will hear your own I AM voice of love speak to you in these words.

I Love You,

Diadra

Debbie "Diadra" Price

CHAPTER 1

TRUST ME!

I AM the Lord of your being, and I speak to all of you who have been yearning and feeling my Presence in your heart. The Lord, your God, is calling you home. All that you have been seeking and yearning throughout the years of your life is now coming into the Kingdom of God.

Trust now, as you read these words, that the voice that you hear in your own heart is the Lord of your being bringing to your remembrance that which was written there long ago.

It is written in your own heart: you are a child of the Most High God. This is what you remember, but have forgotten. So long ago, when you were a little one, you remembered, but then life brought into your world so many things that clouded the vision of my dream in you. How often have you cried for Me? How often have you heard my voice, and yet you could not hear me as I AM.

On the day that you were born in this lifetime, a new world was born inside your soul. This world is now coming into being. It is the light world of truth. This truth has lived within you from the beginning of your life. It started many,

many, many years ago. Long before you ever remember.

I have sent to you many signs, and you did not see them. I have been with you all along. I have spoken. I have heard. I AM there, and always have been. Your soul is yearning for my voice. Hear it now as you read, for I AM you, and you are me, and we are one. There is no separation. I AM you! You are me! We are one!

It is written in your heart: you must go into the world now to be a being of light. I AM dreaming my world through you. Go and touch where you feel me lifting you into another realm of peace. Go and touch where you feel me stirring in your heart. Go and touch where you think I AM to be. Go and touch where I send you. The world needs your touch, for I touch the world through you. So much to be understood, and yet so little time.

Come to me in prayer and meditation. Listen in the stillness of the silence of your soul. Here you will hear my voice as I AM, and I will whisper to you the secrets of the universe and the knowing of your beginning. Do not be afraid to come. Do not be afraid to hear my voice. Do not be afraid. Lo, I AM with you always.

Soon you will begin a mighty work. The work will be the work of the Christ--the work of the indwelling Lord of your being in which you live, move and have your being. You are in the center of this Presence. You are never separated from it.

You will undergo many trials; many dark nights of the soul. Many roads will be traveled, and many tears will be shed, but your hunger and your thirst will bring you home. Here I will be able to feed you, and you finally will be satisfied and completed in the soul of life.

Do not be afraid to travel the roads. Do not be afraid to climb the mountains. Do not be afraid to walk in the shadows, for lo, I AM with you always.

It is written in your heart: you are the beloved child of God. There is none other but this child. This child dwells within the heart of every living soul in this earth. It makes no difference what religion, what race, what country, what language you speak. It makes no difference. You are my beloved child. I live in the heart of every child, and here I speak the truth that you have so longed to hear. Listen carefully now as you read, and I will speak to you.

There is a beautiful light shinning deep within your soul. You have craved the light for a long, long time. You seek it in everything you do. You crave the light in your home. You seek to stand in it whenever you can find it near. You desire only that which is pure. You wish to feel this light all the time, and yet it seems so far away.

The winters of your soul have covered the light, and the light cannot penetrate through the darkness. But it will shine, and you will feel it every moment of your life. Do not be afraid to come into the light. Be willing to let go of every fear. Be willing to turn within and listen to the darkness, for the darkness is nothing. It comes and it goes, and it comes and it goes. It is nothing. Walk in the path of the nothing, and you will find the light. Here I will speak, and here I will guide you into all truth. Face the nothing, and I will show you the way.

When you are afraid, hold that which is dear to your heart. Hold it in your hand and offer it to my hand. I will lead you by the hand into the Kingdom of God. There are times when you will be afraid. There are times when you will be very brave. Do not worry, for either way I AM there. There is no need to be afraid.

It is written in your heart: come unto me all who labor, and I will give you rest. My yoke is easy, and my burden is light. Do you understand this piece of scripture my child? Do you not see that I have been calling you to give me your burdens, to let me carry the load, to let me do the work? And yet, you insist in doing it on your own. Hear me now, if you have not heard me before. My yoke is easy, and my burden is light.

I will carry you the rest of the way if you will give unto me all of the darkness, all of the fear, all of the hurt, all of the tears, all of the things that make you a child of that which you are not.

Trust me now. Trust me with your pain. Trust me with your dark night of the soul. Trust me on the path. Trust me in the mountains. Trust me in the valleys. Trust me...trust me!

It is written in your heart: you do not walk alone. There are many beside you to help you on the way--those whom you know and those whom you don't know. The love of God reaches into the realms of spiritual beingness which you cannot understand. The celestial are all seeking to bless you with the light. Your prayers are heard multidimensionally and reach forth into the universe of Christed beings seeking to bless you on your way.

There is nothing that you need that will be denied you. From here on out the way is clear. Will you not come and ride with me upon the cloud of truth? This truth will carry you into the rain and into the light. It will carry you into the far country and back into God's house. It will carry you into the desert, and it will carry you into the clear waters of the crystal lakes. It will carry you wherever you need to go in order to find your way home to me.

I AM the way; I AM the Truth; and I AM the life. No one comes to God but by me. You have not understood this in the past, but now it will be made clear. I AM the way. I AM the Truth. I AM the life. I AM you, and you are me, and we are one. Does the scripture not tell you this truth? Look it up for yourself in John 14:20. Look it up for yourself. Do you see it written there?

There is only one way to enter into the Kingdom of

God, and that is by pure surrender. Pure surrender means a pure heart, and that is why the scripture promises that you will see God if you are pure in heart. Do you understand what a pure heart means? Take this one deep into meditation and ask me to express to you what is the meaning and the fruit of these words. I will bless you with an understanding that is far greater than you can now even imagine. Blessed are the pure in heart, for they shall see God. Do you understand?

How have we been so far apart? It seems like such a mystery when we are so very close. You have dreamed dreams, have you not? I was there in your dreams, and yet you could not find me. I AM here now in this dream, and yet you cannot find me. How can it be that we are so far apart, and yet you know that I AM you, and you are me, and we are one. How can it be that we are so far apart?

There is only one way to enter into the kingdom of God, and that is to build a bridge -- a bridge between this life and the one that you think you live. Come into God's house with thanksgiving. This begins the bridge ... the bridge of entering in. Thanksgiving in the heart of the child of God is a vibratory energy of great power. It reaches into the realms of the truth and sets you free. Here you will see me as I AM, through a thankful and grateful heart. I AM the bridge. Remember ... I AM the way, the truth and the life.

There is only one Presence and one power in the

universe. That Presence and power is God. In God we live, move, have our being -- closer than breathing, nearer than hands and feet. Are these not words that are so dear to your heart? Why do you think they are so dear? Have I not been with you always? Have I not been reminding you of this truth? Be still, Sweet Angel Child, and listen to these words. Listen to them until they ring their true message within the soul...the very depth of your soul...the deepest aspects of your remembrance.

I will come to you. I will come to you in your dreams. I will come to you in the days. I will come to you in the nights. You must listen for my voice everywhere, for I live everywhere. I live in all time and all space. I live in no time and no space. I AM all there is. I AM!

There is only one Presence and one power, God the good. I AM that Presence and that power. You cannot be separated from me in any way. I AM not afraid. You are not afraid. Everything else is an illusion of fear, and fear carries its own dream. You must awake, Oh Sleeper, and arise from the dead.

It is written in your heart: the journey from here on will be carefully guarded. You will be protected. You are coming home, and I AM drawing you near. If you will relax and take the sabbath of the day and the night, I will take you home quickly and easily back into God's house. If you resist my pull, the way is hard and the road is narrow. I will take you there, if you will come surrendering your will and your way and your life to me.

When you call, I answer. I have always answered your call. Even in the deep, deep experiences of darkness within your soul, never fear, my Precious One, I have still answered. You have just not understood. The connecting link between us has been so very fine, and the voice that speaks within you is so very soft.

Never be afraid to call me. I AM on the other end. We are connected by a bond of eternal love, and this eternal love is what makes me answer your call. I AM the way. I AM the truth, and I AM the life. Study this scripture often. Let it live in your heart, and you, too, will know the way, the truth and the life. The truth within these words will set you free. Then I will be able to call you, and you will be home.

It is written in your heart. Many, many times you have thought that you came to me--calling me, asking, seeking, knocking--but it was I who was calling you, knocking on your door. Behold, I stand at the door and knock. Do you understand?

It is written in your heart. It is, written in your heart, and here the scrolls will be unveiled. The scrolls will be opened. The scrolls and the seals will be broken. You must come unto me. You must come unto me. As you come unto me, this builds the bridge. This builds the bridge and creates the stepping stones upon which you will reach the Presence of who you are.

I AM the way. I AM the truth. I AM the life. But you say, you have already read this so many times in this chapter. My Beloved, read it again, and again and again. Let me read it in you. Let me, read it in you. You are the way. You are the truth. You are the life. You come to God by way of yourself, your true Self--the way, the truth, and the life. There is no other way. There is no other truth. There is no other life. This is what is written in your heart.

I AM you. You are me. We are one. You know this, and as you read this the God bumps of life move in and through your system. You feel the chills upon your head. You feel your heart pounding rapidly. You feel this truth. I AM only bringing to your remembrance that which is written in your heart.

Do not be afraid. Again, do not be afraid. There is a peace like a river flowing at the very center of your being. It has no beginning and it has no end, for it comes from the Source and returns to the Source. Flow in this river of life. Let me take you where I will, and you will find yourself returning to the Source.

This is a good illustration of how to visualize in meditation. See yourself in the river, in the river of life...eternal life. I will bring you home. Rest! Float! Float in the river. Let me carry you where I will. Let me carry you where I will.

Have no fear. You will not drown. I will carry you through the reeds and the rushes. I will you carry through the storms. I will carry you through the streams and the rivers. I will carry you through the oceans. I will carry you home. You are the child in the basket. You are the child in the basket.

It is written in your heart: do not be afraid; for lo, I AM with you always. My words, you see, are written in your heart. You will find them in the scriptures. Look for them there. You will find them in your heart. You will hear them in your prayers. These truths will bring your remembrance back and help you to find your way home. This is the map. This is the way. This is the bridge.

So often you have come. So often you have cried. So often you have asked. So often you have sought. So often you have knocked. The door is opening now, so be at peace. Do not be afraid.

When you wish upon a star, it makes no difference who you are. I will fill your dreams. I will fill your dreams. I AM you, you are me, we are one. Come, my Beloved Star Child, let us go home together.

CHAPTER 2

SELF REFLECTION

I AM mother mirror, because I reflect to you all that you are and all that you are not. The ego is a master of deception. Always remember that. Always remember that. It is a master of deception.

I AM the Christ, and I AM the revealer of all truth through the Holy Spirit. I AM the master of truth. When you call on my name, I will call out the master of the ego.

Trust is everything. Always remember this. Willingness to trust me is everything. You cannot get through the gate without these two. Always remember that.

It is written in all of your hearts, the truth that will set you free in my name. That is why the name, Jesus Christ, is the only name. Live in this name. Immerse yourself in it. Claim it as your divinity in whichever way you are guided to, but claim it as your divinity. Live in my name. Live in it ... live in it. It will take you to all the truth. But mother mirror will also reveal every lie. You are the light of the world, but you cannot see it when you stand in your own shadow.

It is written that we are all one, and that is why you must all sacrifice yourself for one another. This is what it means to love one another as Christ loves you. It is written, "thou shalt have no other gods before me," but you do when you stand in your own shadow. I AM the way. I AM the truth, and I AM the life. It is written, "ye are gods." How many times do I have to tell you I AM with you always, but you will not listen.

If you will give your hand to me, I will take you through the valleys and the shadows. Only when you go through the shadows can you see the light. Have no fear. Love is all there is. I AM with you always. I bring only love, but you must take my hand. This is Grace. I cannot make you give me your hand. You have to stretch it out yourself.

When you were young, you girded yourself and you walked where you would, but when you are old, you will stretch forth your hand and another will gird you and take you where you don't want to go. You must go through the shadow.

If you will follow me, I will take you down the road of life, but I promise you the way is very narrow. Listen to your heart. Always listen to your heart. Blessed are the pure in heart; they shall see God. If your heart is not pure, I will cleanse it, but you must follow me.

Dear Beloved Children, I love you with an everlasting love, but you must trust me. You have so much willfulness, you won't let anything go. It is not yours at all...it all belongs to God.

If you are seeking the Kingdom and cannot find it, you must turn the key. Because you locked me out, you must turn the key and let me in. From this day forward, surrender everything to me...everything. There is nothing left for you to do now but this. It is the last step before you can turn the key.

You are my beloved children, and I love you with an everlasting love. The Christ in every single one of you shows the other one the way. You don't understand this now, but you will.

In my Father's house are many lands. You must travel them alone, but you are never alone, for I AM with you always. Such is the way of the Tree of Life. You have been seeking this wisdom for so long. Close this book, and let my Dove of Peace teach you now!

CHAPTER 3

LOVE IS WHO YOU ARE!

I AM within you, and you are within me. We are one. I AM you, and you are me. We are one. Love is all there is, my Beloved. Love is who you are.

You are on a journey, seeking the love that you are. This, above all else, is what you yearn to know. There are times when you seek to find me, and you do not find me. There are times when you seek to know me as I AM, and you cannot know me. There are times when you seek to be the love of God, and yet you do not feel it. There are times when you know that I AM guiding you, and yet you are not sure.

Such is the pathway back into God's house. The house is the center of love where I AM, and here you must find me. Only when you find me at the center will you know me as I AM and be able to go and to come into God's house at will. The path and the journey into God's house is not an easy one, but it is a journey of love, and you must trust me on this.

The journey of love has many pockets of darkness and shadow, and yet it is the only way home. Love is ALL there is, and love is the way, the truth and the life. It is written, I

AM the way, the truth and life. I AM love, and love is the way, the truth and the life. And so the journey, Beloved, is a journey of love, and only through this journey can you find me...that which you seek to know with all your heart.

Very often you will feel the call of my voice asking you to come to the center to find me there. You will feel it as the desire in your heart to know me. This desire will not leave you alone, and when you feel this call, you must come. It is my will and my way that you would come when you do NOT feel this call, and in this way your journey will be made so much easier.

If you seek me in the silence, in the peace and in the times of no tribulation, the path and the journey through the soul to the house of God will be so much easier and brighter. I AM the way and the truth and the life, and I will guide you through the call or through the silence. You must come, Beloved. You must come, for it is written in your heart that you are the love of God; for I AM the love of God, and I AM you, and you are me, and we are one.

When you give yourself to me in the search and ask me to do the search for you, then I will draw you through the Kingdom and into the glory of God's presence without you taking any thought.

I AM speaking through you now, and I AM loving you as you read these words. The call of love is being felt at the very center, and there is an energy that is being released.

That is because you are feeling that which is written in your heart.

If you would know me as I AM--the way, the truth and the life that leads to the path of love--then you must come to me in the silence and in the peace. Do not wait for the tribulations of the earth to draw you near, for this is the pathway of trial and suffering. Come to me in the silence and in the peace, and I will take you home on the wings of the Great White Dove that lives in your own heart.

I AM the Great White Dove. Therefore, you are the Great White Dove. I would ask that you let me lift you upon my wings and take you home in the silence and in the peace. Do not wait for the trials and the tribulations to draw you into God's house, for again, I assure you, it is the way of darkness, and it is not an easy path.

If you will come to me in your silence and in your peace, you will see that I AM the light, and I AM the truth, and I AM the way. I will teach you every step of the way. You will feel my presence, and you will know the light that shines along the path that draws you near. Then, when the trials and the tribulations come, you will still be able to see my light, and my way, and my truth.

There is a center at which I live. It is the center of the heart. You must find this center in your stillness, for only in this center is the entrance to God's Kingdom made known. This center is beyond all tribulation. It is beyond all darkness.

It is beyond all chaos. It is beyond all that you even consider to be known at present. It is the center out of which all life flows. It is the center out of which you live. It is the center out of which I AM you, you are me, and we are one.

I love you with an everlasting love through this center. Only until this center is found and opened within your own heart will you be able to be the love that for so many centuries you have sought to find. You have sought me in the love of others. You have sought me in the desire to have others love you. You will not find me there. You can only find me at the center of your own heart. When you find me there, you will be the love that you have always sought to find.

In your journey home, you must trust that I know the way, and the way that I choose for you is not the way that I choose for your brother or your sister, or your mother or your father, or even your dearest friend. It is the way that is right for you. It is the way that only you can come, because you have gone out of God's house in your own way, and you can only find your way back if I guide you the way through which YOU came. Do you understand? The way through which YOU left! Do you understand?

I AM the way, and I AM the truth. I will not steer you wrong, and I will not take you from the path. Often, in times of trial and tribulation, you have stepped off of the path of the journey home, but now you have no choice. You feel my call at the center of your heart, and you know that you must return; for the time is drawing nigh, and it is soon to be over. You must make the journey now!

Love me with all your heart. This is all that is required, my Beloved. It is written in the commandment, and you know this is true. But, to love me with all of your heart, you must desire to know me with all your heart. This desire can only be experienced through your longing and through your desire to know me as I AM. I will take you to this center where you will know me, and the desire of your heart will be fulfilled.

You are never to question the way in which I draw you, nor the path, nor that which you see upon the path; for as you go through the return journey, you must understand that many things are to be revealed, and much is to be healed. As you center yourself in the love that draws you through the journey, through the path and through the way, you must trust that whatever you see, and whatever you behold, is my gift of love.

You have been given a great command, and that is to love me with all of your heart. This you cannot do until your heart is pure, and your heart cannot be pure until you find me at the center. You must seek me at the center always.

Love is the center, and I AM the way. Trust that I know the way to bring you to the center, but you must make the commitment to come unto me to be in the presence of my love as I walk you through the journey.

As we walk together back into God's house, I will guide you in ways of service that you do not understand now. All that is required of you is your willingness to be out of control and to have my will done in you. This is the only way to stay upon the path.

I AM truth, and I AM life. These two terms have almost become a cliche in your mind. Yet, they are the greatest words that are written, for through the truth you are guided into the light. Through the light you are guided into the love. Through the love you are guided into eternal life. Only in eternal life will you be able to know me as I AM; for I AM the eternal love that you are. All else is just a mirage.

Love me with all your heart, and then you will know me as I AM. The only way to love me with all your heart is to surrender all that you think you are. Everything is based upon surrender now. This is the map. This is the way. You must surrender all. As you surrender all, the love that you are begins to well up within you, and only then, with this love, can you love me with all your heart. Do you understand?

There is no other way in the life of your being but to come unto me. Whenever you seek me with all of your heart, you must do so with a mind that says I let go and I let you be you in me. You must feel your whole body sinking into the surrender of eternal life. You must rest in the assurance that I will draw you and take you safely into God's house.

You must have no fear as you go and as you walk upon the path, as I take you and lead you and guide you. Many things will be shown to you that you do not believe now. You must trust with all your heart that this is part of the will and the work of the Holy Spirit.

The Holy Spirit is the Great White Dove that lives within your heart, that is quickened and takes flight at my command. Upon the wings of this Dove will you journey home, if you will let it be. The journey is a peaceful one, but you must trust the Holy Spirit or it will not be peaceful.

The Holy Spirit will bring you into God's Kingdom. The Holy Spirit will fly. The Holy Spirit will rise. The Holy Spirit will sing in you.

As you go through this journey, there may be storms along the way. The storms are those thoughts, feelings and emotions that have rained upon your life for centuries, that which is not in alignment with the Son in you. Let the Son shine, but you must be willing to go through some of the rain.

CHAPTER 4

PEARLS OF WISDOM

The winds of time carry you where they will. Supported by the love of God, the wind blows and supports the love. So rest Little Ones. Rest upon the wind with every breath. Love gives birth in the wind. A child is born here. Then gaze with your eyes into the eyes of the children of God.

Enter into the chambers of your heart with every breath. A spiral of light will carry you to the center of your heart. The light lifts when rain comes, falling through the spiders web but never breaking the threads that unite the home of God.

Jesus Christ walked upon the earth in the sands of time and left behind the star dust that fell upon the fertile ground. Gather the sands from the sandals, and let each grain rest in your heart much like a grain of sand in the oyster's home. In the silence of the sea in which the oyster lives, a pearl of great price is born. Master Teacher in the pearl releases the wisdom of the ages--pearls of wisdom unlocking inner revelations in time.

Go often to the water's edge. Observe the coming and

the going of the tides, for here you will find the grains of sand upon which the Master walked. Dive deep into the ocean waters of your soul. Let the waves carry you in and out, in and out. In upon the shore, and out to the sea. In to love's earth plane and out to the sea of eternal life. In to earth and out to sea. In to earth and out to sea. Resist not the waves, nor the water's edge. Look for the pearls in the grains of sand. Become the master of your gaze. Focus only on the pearl. Let the shell fall away. It has served it's purpose.

The voice of wisdom must be heard with the heart. Listen not, listen not with your head. Ask me to open your heart. I AM there. Again, I remind you. I AM the way, I AM the truth, I AM the life. I AM the seed, I AM the Son. I AM you, you are me, we are one! Awake, Oh Sleeper, arise! Come unto me! Bring only your empty shell.

Loving kindness fills your emptiness and overflows into the waters of the earth. Loving kindness heals the empty shell and seeds the waters of the new earth. Loving kindness is the pearl of great price resting upon the shores of your heart.

These keys unlock the Kingdom of God within you. Trust only love. It is the master key to the many mansions in God's house. Throw all the other keys away. This is the one that opens all the doors from this day forward; for all the other keys are literally absorbed in the one.

Thus we continue with the greatest commandment, to

love the Lord your God with all your strength, with all your might, with all your love and with all your heart. Keep this commandment to love. It is the key to all the doors in your Father/Mother's house. As each door opens, another will be revealed, until you reach the stairway of the King's chamber in the pyramid at the center of the Holy Temple of God's house. Remember, the key that opens the door is love. If you come into this chamber with anything in your hand other than this key, you cannot remain. This is the arc of the covenant.

At the pyramidal point of the pyramid in the King's chamber, time stands still. This is the beginning of your remembrance of eternal life. Beyond this point, information cannot be given at this time, for it marks the end of an age, and God alone is the Alpha and the Omega, the beginning and the end of the age.

CHAPTER 5

CHAMBERED NAUTILUS

Listen to your heart every time that you open your mouth, and as you speak you will understand many things. Present to yourself a planner, one who will take notes for you and give unto the world that which you truly believe.

Do not be afraid to speak your truth, for the truth sets you free, whether it be a reality or an illusion. Listen to the heartbeat of the chords of present moments, and soon you will find there is a rhythm of speech that will come through you. Every time you attune to the fork of knowledge, you rest in the wisdom of priests and power.

Personal will often interferes with the voice of truth. Do not be afraid to set this aside and open your mind to love. Personal will often gets in the way of clear messages from the angels within you. If this is the case, understand that your intent of love will always bring your will into alignment with the encasement of the heart's chambered nautilus. Resting here in the chamber often brings about a greater wisdom and understanding so that the voice of the I AM Presence can clearly communicate with the Self that lives upon the earth.

Too many times the individual is prepared to

understand that which has been set into motion at the level of the conscious mind. Very often the conscious mind then dictates to the Spirit the Will and the work. So often this is not in alignment with the great God Self which seeks to make Its' impression through you. Rest in the assurance, however, that your heart's core must be golden. In the golden heart rests the calf of alignment with love.

Trust now that what comes through to you in this alignment of love is within the Will and the work of the Holy Spirit. Trust that everything that is given to you to do at this point of communication is in alignment with the Will, and the work and the divine plan that is written in your heart.

The way that you can tell the difference is a frequency of vibration which brings about an ecstasy feeling. This ecstasy feeling will lift you above the time and space upon which you live in the earth. Do not be afraid to move forward upon this frequency, for as you move upon it, it moves before you also.

Rest in the assurance that God's Will is the impulse of love at the center of all action. When this impulse of love is rested in at the center of the chambered nautilus within the heart, all goes in alignment with the Divine Will, and the way, and the truth and the life of Spirit.

Trust in your Presence to open ways for you and pathways into chambers that are heretofore not known to you. Rest in the assurance that the good Lord knows your will, and knows your work and knows your way. Your will is the will of the work and the way when it is in alignment with the chambered nautilus at the core of the Master Presence within you.

Open your mind and your heart, and be not afraid to enter into these chambers as you dive between the veils of many separations that have occurred in lifetimes hither and yon. Going into unknown chambers of the heart may be scary for the little child who has not been in the diving waters before. Often, as the child swims beneath the veil that has been opened at the surface, there are many worlds of fantasy and many worlds of open-heartness.

Our Father/Mother God has endowed within every individual a calligraphy of wonderful truths and blessings to be revealed. Every single cell of life, and that is what you are, is impregnated with many chambers of love. This love chamber fantasizes in many ways and creates a world after its likeness and image upon which the divine imprint has been placed in the beginning.

Try not to compare your chambered nautilus to that of another, for they are not alike. Each chamber within the individual cell is single and one, and one of great beauty. Diversity of the Life Force is the nature of Father-Mother God at the center of all cell life. Knowing this, you can become a center point of love and light in the calligraphy of life.

Rest in the mindset that all is within you, and that you need look nowhere else for any of your instructions. Housed within the inner chambers of the nautilus is the word and the power and the energy that will carry forth and bring into manifestation God's plan.

Go forth now into your world, and rest in the chamber of the heart in which you breathe...in which your breathe...in which you breathe. Rest in the breath, and rest in the breath, and rest in the breath. Upon the wings of the breath you will be carried deeper into the chamber; and every time you penetrate into a nautical newness, you will understand, sooner or later, the Will and the work of the Holy Spirit as it is impregnated within you. Trust now that this Spirit is an omniscient one in which all is known and all is well.

Love is at the center of every impulse of this divine calling. Every time you say "yes" unto the calling, coming into the chamber you will be given a message whether or not it registers in the upper chambers of the mind.

Strings of wisdom are like threads in the tapestry of the many mansion worlds within you. You are sewn together with seams of a mighty Presence. Calling forth your I AM Presence is a powerful activity that requires much peace. Listen to your heart and the chords of love resonating with the peace of God. These are the strings of the heart.

Beloved Angels, knowing is a part of becoming. Follow your sounds to the matrix of eternal Omness. Trust in the Om that bursts forth from the middle. Become the Presence with this sound in your mind, and follow the vibration of the sound deep ... deep ... deep.

Every tone echoes through the ethers of time, making arrangements for your memory to expand. Trust in the wisdom revealed. Question not with reasoning. The inner levels of listening are not like that of the conscious mind. These levels of listening move in waves and particles. They burst forth light and fill the cells of the soul. Know not from where they come, and question not where they go. They are disbursed on the wings of the Dove. The homing device within the Dove carries the vibrational frequency to the needed parts of the many selves of the One.

Listen now to the vibrational frequency as the Om speaks and sings and resonates from your heart. Allow the modulation of the voice to be carried by the intonation of the impulse at the center of the Om. The divine intelligence at the center of the impulse will carry the toning to the degree of intensity and volume that is needed for your soul. Love is the frequency of the toning. God is the impulse of the frequency. Preserve your time in stillness. Love is the only Presence and power, centered in the I AM of God.

In the quickening of God's heart, the almightiness of the true Self is scattered upon the creations of the many mansion worlds. The good Lord, in His building, establishes the Kingdoms in the many mansions of time. Only the heart that is quickened by the light frequencies of the I AM Presence can begin to co-create with the power of the I AM in the purity which it was meant to express.

Follow your dream, for this is the wave length and the particle that connects you with the Source at the center of the chambered nautilus unfolding and deepening within you. The dream comes to you upon a wave of liquid light impulsed at the center of wisdom and love, merging in the twin flames that unite them in wholeness. Love and wisdom, united in wholeness, create God's world and bring into manifestation the Kingdom of God in the earth.

Coming into the light will enable you to see with the heart. The eye of the heart is single. Mustard seeds are sown through the single eye, and they carry the co-creative energy of love and wisdom as they are scattered by the omniscience, the Will and the work at the center of the seed.

Be willing to be the sower, the reaper, the nurturer and the bringer of the dawn upon the seed; for created in the image of our Father-Mother God, the light frequency resides within you as the quickening agent in the earth.

Many times you have entered into creative processes with the Father/Mother, Elohim God. Many dimensions of creation have been experienced by many of you. Do not judge this one.

Free yourself from preconditioned ideas that have been placed in your heart through the reading of many books.

The wisdom of co-creation rests within you, for here it was written in the beginning. The Alpha and the Omega bursts forth the seed, impulsed by the love and wisdom frequencies of pure light. As they go forth released in you, mighty work is accomplished in this particular mansion.

Lullaby

Be not afraid. Be not afraid. Come into the light.
Love is the key. Open up the door. Turn it with your will.
Presence now. Resting still, opens the cradle of love.
Rest my child. Rocked by love. Still in the heart of God.
Come my child. Rest awhile. Sleep in the silence of love.
Go in peace upon the earth. This is your mother's child.
Rest awhile. Rock my child, in the cradle of love.
Give your heart and your mind to your Father and Mother.
Listen still. Wind will blow, rocking your cradle to and fro.
Be not afraid, rest in the wind. I AM, blowing you home.

Infinity swirls in every cell. Image and likeness of God swirls in infinity. Meditate upon the figure eight. This is the river of life. Wisdom will be gained by floating in the river of life. Listen to the movement of the river. The sound of the waves carry within them the secret of the mystery of the Kingdom within you. Meditate upon the symbol of infinity. Otherwise, you will not understand these words.

Coming together in the hearts of so many of God's

children is the wisdom and the love captured in infinity. They cannot move beyond the boundaries of the personal will however; therefore, surrender the personal will into the symbol for eternity. The Will of God opens the windows of the chambers of the nautilus. Open your heart. Open your heart. Listen! Listen! Listen!

Here is the way that you may know when you hear what you are listening for. You will begin to feel a sense of open-minded listening, as if your mind and your heart are being stretched to capacity creating empty spaces. In the empty spaces, there will be for you an infusion of liquid light which moves with the rhythm of the infinite Merkabah. As the infusion occurs, you will begin to feel a frequency or an intense vibration that is foreign to you in the present state. Some of you will feel it as a blissfulness; others as a mighty rush of energy. To some, waves of peace will engulf you. To others, it will feel like a gentle rain filling the empty spaces.

After the infusion, your faith will grow in strength. Faith in the love of Christ within you will expand. Your peace will become more of your every day experience, and you will move with great poise and power. You will begin to reach out to serve, impulsed by a divine love growing inside of you that cannot be denied.

The compassion for your fellow travelers will fill your heart so full that you must serve your neighbor, your brother, your sister. Love will engulf you to such an extent that you will not know yourself. You will begin to receive greater and greater guidance and wisdom with stronger frequencies of assuredness. The impulse to move will become a very conscious impulse that moves you, literally, to greater good.

People will begin to understand and feel the love and the wisdom and the truth that is living you. You will rest upon the rock of Peter's faith, and the waters and the wind will not disturb you.

You will be called upon in the night to embrace your fellow travelers. You will be called upon in the day to carry them in your cradled heart.

Very often, you will be sent to where you do not understand, and you will hear yourself say and do many things that to your conscious mind makes no sense.

Love born in the heart is the wisdom of God, and cannot be judged by the human mind. Your impulse to move and serve will begin to stretch you and bring you to a higher pentacle for an even greater deepening ... an even more powerful experience of the infusion of the light waves. Rest in the assurance that each impulse is a divine impulse of love, stretching your beingness to fulfillment.

Do not be concerned with other's opinions. They will not understand. Finding yourself in places of judgement is a call from your spiritual I AM Presence to love. You will be used in many ways and many places, for love seeks out the darkness as darkness seeks out the light. Understand that love is a frequency of light that draws the darkness and absorbs it unto itself. It is the magnet of the co-created world that keeps everything in balance and co-creation.

Clear your mind and your heart daily, giving it a bath of silence. For every day, as you go forth from the bath, you will begin to accumulate the dust of the earth again. You must bathe often as you begin to be used by the infinity expanding in you.

Care not for your own life. Care not with anxiety for anything. Let the life within you care for you and for everything in the earth.

Troubled waters respond to a call from the center point of infinity when you speak the word of peace. And so, to the troubled waters in the earth, continue the message, "Peace be still". Enter into the word, and then speak it from the center point of the infinity and eternal life within it, resting in your heart; for it is here that it is written.

Compelled by love, you go forth into the winds of time. Written in your heart is an eternal Book of Life that is being read to you page by page. Sit with the Book of Life within you. Allow the pages to be turned by the I AM Presence who is the author. You must come to it with a willingness to have the pages read, and again, only at the center of the infinity of silence will you be able to see the written word.

Combinations of information will come together to

synthesize the divine plan -- the plot, the theme, the purpose, and the message that is written in your Book of Life. The earth is a tremendous library of collections and annotations of God's Will. Each individualization of the cellular Life Force has within it written the Book of Life, titled completely different and written for a new purpose. As you sit with your Book of Life, the seals of time will be broken, and, thus, you will move from chapter to chapter until you have completed the work.

Always remember, the author breaks the seals, and so you must rest at the center allowing this impulse to quicken the energy necessary for this cellular breaking.

Some of you will begin to hear and feel the Will of God speaking in tones of remembrance. To you, it will seem as though you have read this book before. Naturally so, for it was written in the beginning. To some of you, many of the chapters will seem a mysterious adventure, as though you have never read this adventure before. This is the Will of God, that you discover it anew for the first time, even though it was written long ago in the beginning.

Do not judge whether you feel remembrance or awaking, for that is a matter of perception, given to the one as part of the Divine Plan for the fulfillment and the completion and the unfoldment of the eternal Tree of Life that is written in your heart.

Only God understands the mysteries within the book.

God's Will cannot be comprehended by the human mind, but it can be brought to a point of awareness through willingness and surrender. Therefore, make no judgements upon yourself or your fellow travelers as the chapters unfold and reveal the Divine Plan of love.

CHAPTER 6

OMNI ASHNI!

Omni Ashni! Omni Ashni! These are words that can be taken into the heart. Repeated with reverence, they will bring forth a consciousness of love and peace. They come from ancient manuscripts long ago forgotten, and they need to be remembered in the hearts and the souls of humankind. Omni Ashni!

Prepare the mind with these words, for they will help to unlock the doors of the inner chambers of the indwelling spiritual heart. As these words penetrate into the etheric realms of the spider's web within, new dimensions of wisdom and understanding will surface in the mind.

Take these words deep to your center, both day and night, resting with them in consciousness. Trust that what is going on is beyond the mental comprehension, and that there is a resonant frequency of light being expanded in the cellular structure of the physical, mental and emotional bodies.

After completion of meditation upon these words, rest in the silence. In moments of peace, you will understand many things coming from a dimension of yourself known to you as the Christ. This will open the chamber of the heart, moving your awareness to deeper mansions in God's house.

Together we come into God's house in this way--one by one, meditating upon **Omni Ashni**. And yet, as you come into God's house one by one, you quicken the Life Force in the whole earth's population, and, thus, you truly enter, two by two.

Rest in the assurance that these words have contained within them the secret doctrine of the ages. Listen patiently and quietly, resting in the cradle of the vernacular of these terms, and soon you will begin to feel a new frequency of love pouring through the veins of the soul.

Open your mind and your heart to be empty of all thoughts except these two words, and, one day in the near Son future, you will understand the true essence of their power. These words are given to you from the heart of the I AM Temple within you, and they come with love and peace.

Encoded in the soul of the human personality there resides a memory that was placed there long ago by the Father/Mother Shekinah, the everlasting I AM Presence of God. This Presence of love is written in the heart of all humankind, presenting Itself into awareness through unlocking many chambers in the heart.

The impulse of love is the most powerful transforming force in all of the universal systems of God's Kingdom. It is the uniting force that spins a web from universe to universe, unlocking many, many lifewaves joining you together in One

... in One ... in One!

Presently, you will begin to understand that life is multidimensional and, upon the planes of Spirit, you rest in many ways and in many forms. The complexity of your beingness reaches the farthest star of your galaxy, and the presence of love that you are moves even beyond dimensional worlds of reality known to humankind.

Many lifewaves of beings are filtering your planet with this same love frequency that is now birthing itself through the inner nautical chambered heart frequency of the one Presence and power known as the principle of Jesus Christ. Enter ye now into this principle through the power of the words "Omni Ashni." Omni Ashni will awaken in you the love vibration of Jesus Christ and fulfill the mission that is written in your eternal heart.

Love is all there is, and it is written in the cells of all life forms. The structure of its components is not known to the human consciousness, nor will it ever be revealed at the human awareness level. As love is quickened in the entire structure of the human being, it alone will reveal the higher teachings of wisdom that come forth from the magnetic quality of this vibratory energy.

The mind is the energy of God's intelligence, but the heart is the wisdom of the love center coded in the heart of God. Rest in the assurance that as this center is quickened by the frequency contained in Omni Ashni, there will be revealed upon the earth a new age. After you have meditated upon the Omni Ashni words for a time frequency that is perfect for you ... and you will know this time frequency, then you will begin to understand and be given instructions of a higher nature.

The Age of Enlightenment is now coming to an end, and the Age of Ascension is upon us. Enlightenment always leads to ascension, which is simply a rising above, in and through the frequency of light. In the ascension process, humankind will understand more of the global unity and the compassion that awaits the opened heart.

Humankind will soon understand the power of the universal Om, and the understanding will penetrate into many mansion worlds to be revealed and helped into manifestation.

Listen with the still small voice in the center of the chambered nautilus of the heart, and, if you will listen with the still small voice within this chamber, you will begin to recognize it as your very own.

Trust in the messages that come through, even though they do not appeal to the reasoning molecules of your mind. The reasoning molecules function in you for the purpose of enlightenment. They have brought you to a new peduncle soon to be penetrated by a higher frequency of love. This frequency of love is empowerment to ascension, and it is the next step in the evolution of humankind.

You will soon be brought into a new dimension and school of light that will teach the principles of co-creation from an understanding not yet comprehended by the human mind. Schools of thought are now being collected in the galaxy of light bearers and are being transmitted to some of you through the love frequency. As you pick up these materials to read, you will know that they are from the Christ home. The Christ home is where the children of God birthing the Jesus Christ Consciousness reside.

When you pick up these materials, you will automatically understand and know, through the vibration that you feel in your body as you read, that they are from the frequency of Jesus Christ love. These materials will help you; and by doing, and reading and participating in the experience of the written word, you will begin to feel changes in your mind and in your heart. If you do not feel these changes quickening you to a greater capacity for loving, then you will know that they are not of the New Earth.

Perhaps you have questioned many of the things you have been reading and wondering whether to believe this or to believe that. Again, I caution you that reasoning with the mind does not work in the birthing of this new love. You must read with your heart. You must listen with your heart. You must rest in your heart, and only through your heart will you know the truth that will set you free and give you birth in Christ Jesus.

Love is the power that unites the universe. It is the spiritual glue that contains and keeps the children of God in eternal life. The love of Christ resonates and is in the literal veins of consciousness penetrating the planet and the manifest expression of humankind. Powerful transmissions of love are being received by many of you on the earth at this time.

If you will ask in the chamber of the heart for the wisdom that you need for the next step of unfoldment into the ascension realms, then this prayer will penetrate the veils that separate any problem in your life from that coming to pass.

The purity of the heart's prayer is the record that is received on high and the intensity and the purity and the intention of the heart is the measure of the prayer. Remember, the great Master said it is the measure that you give that you receive.

CHAPTER 7

LONELINESS

Loneliness is a part of the separated soul, but it can also be a guiding light to inner transformation. So, if you have felt lonely even in the crowds, know that this is an inner transforming energy that is drawing you into your center. Awakened to this awareness, allow your loneliness to spiral you inward to the resting place of the birthing chamber.

The perception of this energy as lonely is only in the conscious mind, known to you as loneliness. It is a true reflection of the mind's awareness of being separated, which is simply not the truth of your reality. This will be a clue for you that a veil is soon to be rended if you will rest in a state known as alone.

Your love for God and for the Christ companionship will bring you from your inner realization of loneliness to an eternal life realization of union. In this union, loneliness does not exist. It is impossible; for union means one with all, and God is all. Forever comforted in the oneness of the All, your loneliness will disappear from the face of your knowingness.

Rest in the assurance that you are being assisted by love frequency beings of high intensity. You may never see or hear them, for that is not necessary for your inner awareness or awakening. These Light Beings have left loneliness far behind and only know union and communion with God. In this sense of separateness in which you now live, you expect to be spoken to from separateness. This is not the way of the Gathering of Light Beings, for in the gathering there is only the consciousness of oneness.

Included in the instructions in this chapter, I encourage you to be ever mindful of your threefold being -- body, mind and Spirit. The Spirit is the truth that lives in the eternal life of you, and is that which is merging the rest of you into union. As your body and your mind come into spiritual awareness, the mind releases all sense of separation and loneliness. As the body comes into the frequency of the perfect mind, it, too, looses all memory of separation and loneliness. When this memory is forgotten, all is forgiven, and in forgiveness lies the key to ascension.

Past memory contains veils of falsification and manifestations in the earth of the sense of separation. These ideas cannot live in eternal life, for separation does not exist in this awareness. Read this again, Beloved, and you will understand even more.

Ask God for instructions for you. Ask God, not another human being. Another human being may be the instrument through which God gives you some instructions, but come through the arc of the chamber in the heart. This is the doorway to God's Kingdom of instructions.

Your instructions will be made clear, but you must be conscious that God blesses you with instructions in many, many ways. Listen for the inner I AM Spirit of love's prompting, and move to action according to the prompting energy.

Look into the earth for blessings of light that come to release messages from God. Listen in your heart to the spoken words of others and to the music and to the beautiful expressions of life all around you. You have many teachers presenting instructions as the gift of Grace in manifestation through the earth. But always remember to ask for instructions from the Father/Mother God that lives within you.

Once the doorway is opened to the higher chambers of the spiritual Self of you, you will be guided continually without the dry spells; and you will know, and you will not fear, and you will be sent, and you will hear, and you will express your guidance in the earth.

Presence of love always announces Itself with peace. Presence of love always announces Itself with ecstasy vibrations. Presence of love always announces Itself as goodness. There is no desire, nor any understanding of desire, for accumulated possessions in the Presence, and, therefore, all desire for accumulated possessions must be transmuted for the desire for selflessness, and godliness and glory to God.

Become aware of your need and attachments. The experience of need is a call from the inner Self to release and to give that which you think you have need of. Give your need to God through the heart, and God will release from within you the capacity to fill the need from within. You will begin to give that which you thought heretofore you needed, and in the giving will be the receiving, and the whole understanding will be turned right side up. For now, it is upside down.

Many of your concepts are perceived through a glass very darkly. They are clouded perceptions of reality and must be purified and wiped clean in the soul by the Spirit in order to set things and see things aright.

When you are looking through a clouded window, it all seems as shadows, and shadows do not cast the perfect vision of the Perfect One. Again, I encourage you to ask God through the purity and the intent of your heart to clean the windows of your soul.

CHAPTER 8

PRESTANCE

Written in the hearts of the children of God is the tremendous power of love. Rest in the assurance that this love is being made manifest through the vernacular and through the imagery of deep prayer and meditation.

As the student of love becomes welcomed into the chambers of the heart, the Presence of I AM that lives within this place of contentment will release to the student of love the energy of Prestance. Prestance is a subject that is not understood on the planet at this time. Prestance comes from being centered in a chamber not yet quickened of the spiritual energies brought to the surface of the conscious mind. Prestance will become more known as these energies of love quicken the spiritual nature into the lower bodies. Prestance! This word will soon be known by the children of God as the quickening agent or elixir of love.

Captured in the cells of the entire human being is a code of remembrance placed there by the Father/Mother God, Elohim. This elixir of love has been programmed to be activated at the time of the New Age, which is upon us now.

It has taken several aeons of time for this elixir of

love to be activated and to come into being. Consciousness has needed to be increased in complexity through the activity of turning the mind in upon itself.

Prayer and meditation, as the result of the collective consciousness of humankind, has reached a saturation point which enables this elixir of love to be quickened and brought into remembrance.

It has been understood in the galaxies of life that God's creative process does not necessarily go according to the will and the work of the mental of the human being.

Our Father/Mother God is the creative principle of all life, and through the divine selection process of the infinite mind, all that is created has encoded within it the elements and the structure of perfection. The Divine Idea for humankind, known as the Christ Principle, has encoded within it the structure and the elements for perfection. This elixir of love is now coming into being and expressing itself in manifestation as the Divine Love of God.

We are created in the image and likeness of the benevolent, omnipresent intelligence, and contained within the encoded memory of the entire being is that elixir of love that must come forth if the fullness of the expression of God is to be made known and experienced in the earth. Love is the only Presence and the only power that exists in the realm of God Mind. Contained within love is every aspect of creative principle.

As humankind has evolved in the expression of earth, a fully awakened consciousness has been the goal. This has evolved over aeons of time and manifested in the earth's energy atmosphere, and many of you have returned here several times ... several times, more than several...and have become quickened by degree.

The forces of nature have helped in that quickening. The laws of the universe also have been important catalysts for this transformation. Pregnancy with the Life Force through each incarnation enables births to take place that quicken this elixir of love.

Every time you enter into the earth plane's atmosphere, you are given the opportunity to be quickened, and to be transformed and to be brought into the fullness of the love that is encoded within the cellular memory of your being.

Jesus Christ was the fullest example of the perfection made manifest. This is the Divine Idea of the Only Begotten, simply meaning the Presence of God manifesting in human experience.

As you study the teachings of Jesus Christ and implement the action of love that He demonstrated as He walked the sands of the earth, this action becomes the drawing force, the quickening agent, the impulse that brings to the surface the memory of the encoded pattern of perfection. That is why it is imperative that you follow Him.

Follow Him from the birth, through the wilderness and the ministry of love and life; being willing, thus, to go through the crucifixion of all states of awareness of the soul that need to be resurrected into the eternal life pattern of love.

His message of power and peace and love were to leave in the earth the seeds of remembrance that, when identified with the mind and the heart and the action, will call forth the remembrance within the soul of each individual. As each individual is brought into remembrance, the awakened state of one becomes the catalyst for the quickening and the awakening of another. Thus, two by two you enter the arch, the doorway to the Father's Kingdom of Love.

Rivers of life have carried you into many dimensions of experience. All possibilities of manifestation have needed to be understood at the mental, the emotional and the physical levels in order to bring forth this new creative process. Resurrection takes place as the elixir of love is quickened in the soul through forgiveness of the patterns of remembrance that have not been in alignment with the perfection written in the heart of the children of God.

As love is born in the child's heart, the Kingdom of God is enabled to be made manifest through the vibrational frequency of purity that is held in the heart as this is born. Just as with any birth, this new frequency of remembrance must be nurtured in order to be carried forth into expression. It comes into being as a small child groping and reaching for the purest expression of itself, diving into waters yet unknown, exploring the earth and the elements with new eyes and new ears.

This elixir of love is also the quickening agent for the coming together of all of the powers of the soul: faith, love, trust, etc. You will be enabled to trust God, who is invisible in the manifest world in absolute form, at a degree of intensity that has never before been enabled by you to accomplish.

Rest in the assurance that you are not alone as this birthing process of remembrance takes place. Those who have gone before you and been quickened into remembrance are assisting you on every level of your consciousness. This is made possible because of the truism of unity in consciousness that is a program of oneness in the divine principle of the Christ.

Billions of beings are now being brought into the full expression of the inner Self. This ignites a new dimension of race consciousness that enables billions more to enter into the river of life. Every time you enter into the chambers of the heart through the activity of prayer and meditation and devotion, you are drawn into the river of life of this new race mind awareness and, thus, lifted up into a new creature in Christ Jesus. This is not your own doing, but the Grace of God drawing His children back into His house.

Presently upon the planet earth there are many Light

Beings who have been sent. Their purpose and mission is to assist in the lifting of consciousness. As you turn within to the Father/Mother God of your own being, many of you will be guided and directed into the presence of these Light Beings. Because of your oneness, a resonance frequency will be established as was in the time of Jesus Christ, and the healing of the soul will begin to take place in accelerated proportions.

Trust your inner guidance as you are prompted to go hither and yon. As the inner yearning of your heart compels you into devotion and learning and prayer, trust the action and the movements of the physical self as you are impulsed to go forth in the search for God. Never question the impulse to go forth and to reach out. Never question the impulse to withdraw from the world and to enter into the deepest silence of the Self. This becomes the coming and the going in the earth and the Spirit. An inward drawing and an outward expression. Withdraw and enter. Withdraw and enter ... pattern of unfoldment. Go ye into the world and experience the fullness of its beauty. Go ye into the Spirit and experience the fullness of remembrance.

During your time in the earth, you must be prepared for many new ideas to enter into your awareness. As long as you insist on containing only one megabyte, you will not grow in awareness and fulfillment. Allow the wisdom and the elixir of love to stretch the computer of your heart so that you can hold and contain the All of God and, thus, glorify His name.

The wisdom of the entire universe will be released through the memory of your soul, and you will bring into manifestation the divine ideas which will create, in the earth, God's Kingdom.

Many of you will be moved to begin to study the history of the soul and the genetic makeup of the physical body as it is evolving over time through the experience of earth and consciousness. Communication devices now known to humankind will soon become obsolete, for the inter-telecommunication system is now being activated as love bursts forth the remembrance of union.

From universe to universe, the remembrance of this union has taken place, and now it is time for the earth to be embraced in the union of God in remembrance. Earth is welcomed as a conscious entity now residing in the fully awakened Kingdom of God.

Beginning in the year 1994, many transitions will take place as Mother Earth and her children are welcomed into remembrance. Question not the why of the changes occurring in the earth's pattern. Instead, I encourage you to question the places within your heart where you find it difficult to love. Focus not on the changes taking place in the outer, but on the river of life that is beginning to flow in your awareness and in your body.

If you will remember, in the beginning of your study of Christianity the book of Genesis gives a prophecy of eternal life as the promise of partaking of the Tree of Life. Therefore, I encourage you to take the promise of the scripture in Genesis, and now stretch forth your hand, impulsed by your heart, to partake only of the Tree of Life.

The Tree of the Knowledge of Good and Evil was necessary for you to become illumined to the co-creative process possible through conscious awareness. But now, least you stretch forth your hand and partake of the Tree of Life, the world will entropy upon itself. The Tree of Life consists only of the eternal reality of love.

How many times did Jesus emphasize partaking of the tree of love and life? He showed us the way. Practice His teachings until they become such a part of the soul that you forget any other ways. The practice of His teachings find resonance in the megabytes of consciousness and bring to the surface the eternal reality that is known only within your Spirit. Thus, you become fully spiritualized in every expression of your being in the earth: mental, emotional and physical.

As all of you is quickened by the Spirit of you, union with God is inevitable. This union taking place can become very misunderstood, for programmed within your mind is a story of how humankind, at the level of its own understanding, perceives the resurrection and the ascension to be. You must enter into this quickening with an open mind and heart. Thus, become totally empty of past remembering. Bring an empty chalice to the wisdom and the love center within the chambers of the heart.

Becoming empty is a difficult process for the human being, for attachments of fullness have found resonance in the home of consciousness. These attachments have served a purpose for growth, but now they must be released if new wine is to fill the cup.

Practice the Presence of God with every attitude and remembrance of the conscious mind. There are many ways to practice the Presence, and you will be guided as to the tools that will help you practice the Presence as you turn within asking God with your purity of heart, desiring only to glorify the I AM Presence of love.

Devotion is a powerful tool to aid the birthing process of love. Devotion brings the awareness of the mind and the heart together in the manger where Christ is born.

Become a witness to the birth, not an instructor. Stand aside and observe the compassion and the peace and the power at work within you. God's wisdom and strength and benevolence is the deliverer of the Christ child. This immaculate conception can only be witnessed, not implemented.

When at all possible, rest in your labor pains and breathe deeply, thus the birthing process will not be as difficult as if you resist.

Again, I caution you, do not be the director of how the birth will take place. Become the witness and observe. Step aside while God literally brings into manifestation the image and the likeness of Itself.

Glory be to God and to the wonder of His ways. God's power to give birth to Itself can never be grasped by the mind of the created. Only the Creator can understand and know the inner workings of birth. Centered in the chamber of the almighty God, love is born.

Rest in the assurance that the Kingdom of God shall be made manifest in the earth. This is destiny. And though you have free will, destiny will always take precedence. Your free will lies in your capacity to surrender and accept your destiny. Resistance only delays the inevitable choice for eternal life.

Your Father/Mother God has sheep of many folds, and none of them is lost. They may wander away, but God is the all-seeing, all-knowing eye, and He will find you wherever you happen to lose your way.

Turn Beloved, turn. Turn around, turn around, turn around. Lift up your heart in praise and thanksgiving. Rejoice in your days and your moments. The promise of eternal life is written in your heart. It is the destiny of the created child, and that is why Jesus called the little children unto Him. You are being called, through the yearnings of your heart, to know and remember the Christ.

Let not your hearts be troubled, neither let them be afraid. The Christ is with you always. It is birthing you into remembrance of the love that you truly are. Follow your heart. Follow your heart. Follow your dream. Let your mind become the dream catcher, and let your heart give it birth. Be not afraid to step out in faith as the impulse of love quickens you into the Divine Plan for your life.

Question not your guidance. Just listen with your heart and follow the impulse to move. Go where you are prompted to go. Always take the thought of love with you. The catalytic impulse of love is working to draw you into a full remembrance of the Divine Plan that is written in your heart. God alone can fulfill this mission now. So rest my child in the arms of the benevolent One in whom you live and move and have eternal life.

Angels from on high assist you in your awakening process. God has many creations, and this life of love is none the less productive in your process of awakening. They were created from the compassionate heart of God to serve His Kingdom in a process known as joy.

The joy of the angels is to assist you. Their ways of assistance are not known to humankind, but very often their presence can be felt as a lifting power and a peace. Always rest with the angels in sleep, allowing their comfort and their presence to be the messengers of God for hope. They will help to strengthen your faith, for their energy rests in faith alone.

Reaching out with Wings of Spirit, their healing capacity is an incredible graceful gift. Be not afraid to ask for their assistance. It is their job.

Glorify your Lord in every expression of life. Praise God's holy name, and rest in God's Kingdom of love. Go forth into the earth, and claim God's destiny written in your heart. Reach out to your brother and your sister. Become the angels of love in the earth, one to another.

Glory be to God on high. This is the beginning of a new time and a New Earth. This is the beginning of the Tree of Life growing and manifesting and giving of its fruit on the planet known as the Good Earth.

Missions will soon be accomplished by so many of you who are yearning to serve. Rest assured that the yearning of your heart to be used by God is the opening of the Book of Life. And this opening of the Book of Life will guide you to that place of service that will enable you to become a very important participant in the birth of this Christ child in the earth.

Do not question where you are drawn to serve. There are no places of more importance than others. Some of you will be used in silent spots, and some of you will be upon the platforms expressing the truth to millions. Some of you will remain in homes raising the children of God. Remember the mission of Joseph and Mary. Could there have been a more important one in the earth. Go, therefore, into your own mission, knowing that every place of service in the earth is precious to God and the fulfillment of God's divine plan.

I AM you ... are I AM. I AM ... You are I AM!

CHAPTER 9

COMPASSION

You must understand, Dear Ones, that the beginning of the New Age is not about the coming of the Messiah, but about the coming of one that is to help the world move into an understanding of the Messiah within. Each one of you contains within you a beloved I AM Presence that is being born into the earth, and this will carry you into the New Age. When you rest in the assurance of this truth, then your mind will begin to open to a new understanding of what life is all about.

Jesus the Christ came into being to help you understand this great truth. Did He not say I AM within you? "Lo, I AM with you always ... In that day you will know that I AM in my Father, and you in me, and I in you." Read the scriptures carefully and see if you do not find this to be His message.

Rest in the assurance now that His second coming is deeply upon us, and we are moving into the age known as the Christ. This is the Age of Ascension; the age in which we will ascend above the mind and into the realm of the known Presence of God.

Taking EMLA 1-3 months
Go into Silence. Live
off of money
from House
+ 1/08 Taxes

Your mind has a set of remembrances that keep this new understanding from penetrating the veils. You must come into the Presence of your I AM if you would awaken and be able to see this new Messiah in the earth. The Messiah is not a person, but it is the light of God indwelling every man, woman and child. Be assured that the love of God is present in you, and that you, too, are the Only Begotten.

Your Father/Mother God loves you with an everlasting love and is giving this Presence a name in you known only to your I AM Presence. Some of you will begin to receive what you may call a spiritual name. This name is written within your heart as the individualization of the Messiah within you. It is the saving principle that is lifting you out of bondage and into the promised land. Welcome this Messiah within you, and know that this Presence is the love of God that you are.

Rest in the assurance that much ascension is taking place in the earth now in many of the Light Beings of children. Children are coming into the world in a new understanding that has not yet been born in the earth. The quickening of the heart is the new awakening that is taking place among all of the children of God, not just the new Light Beings. As the children enter into the earth's atmosphere, they begin to release the remembrance of who they are, thus quickening the adult population into remembrance before the time of having to make a transition into another world. Thus, we have the beginning of the New Age even now in the earth. So be prepared for the awakening to take place soon.

Turbulence in the earth is the result of the energies of non-compassion. Non-compassion is eruptive and destructive in the cellular memory of Mother Earth. She is bruised and in need of rest from the non-compassion of the human mind. Cradle her in your heart as you awaken to the eternal flame of the vibratory love of Jesus Christ.

Mother Earth is cooperating to the best that she has the ability to do at this time. But again I remind you, she has been deeply bruised and abused. Therefore, she must go through some healing transitions as well as the population of humanity.

God is alive and well in His universe, filling this planet with a regenerative energy that is like a miracle serum going into all of the life cells on every level, from the physical, to the mental, to the emotional, to the cellular of the earth itself. Be assured that this elixir of life is part of the Divine Plan which was sent forth in the very beginning of the divine idea expulsion from God.

As this quickening continues to take place in the earth, many of you will come into alignment with what is known as your Christ Self. This Christ Self is the birth of the newborn Life Force taking you into God's house and bringing you back into arms of love.

Before you, you will find set among the many blessings of this home every good desire of your heart. Therefore, let every good desire of your heart now rest upon the pages of the written word that you so claim in prayer and meditation. Let the desires of your heart be awakening symbols for you of what is to come in the New Earth, and embrace them now, even though they may not appear in manifestation. The love that you generate as you hold the desires in your heart, with acceptance, will help to bring about the banquet table and the feast. Know that God is always ready to present this feast of blessings to you if you will truly open every aspect of your awareness to the acceptance of these treasures.

For now, the time is come upon us that we should enter into a new study of learning. This study of learning is soon to become a light unto many children of God. The new subject of learning is all about the compassionate heart that must be reached in order to extend the arm of God into civilization.

The compassion of Christ is beyond the mental, the emotional and the physical understanding of compassion upon the earth at the present time. The compassion of Christ is a passion of love that is released into the service of all of the beings in the world. This compassion is a passion for life itself, and it reaches into the depths of the understanding heart. This compassion has within it no understanding of separateness, nor does it have any understanding of being caught in the middle of something that is not true. This compassion reaches to the far corners of the earth and embraces the totality of every living thing upon it. It is understood in this compassionate mind awareness that all is one and one is all.

As this compassion is born in the human awareness, the way that animals and the earth elements are treated will completely change. There will be a reaching out among all people to preserve the Life Force in every living thing. As this understanding begins to emerge in the consciousness of humanity, there will be new ways of preservation presented to the awareness of the human mind. Thus, the need for the destroying of the Life Force within the planet to preserve the Life Force in humankind will cease. These new understandings will come through the deepening of the chambers of wisdom as the divine ideas of love and compassion come together.

Listen carefully in the prayer times of your inner Self to messages that may relate to new beginnings and divine ideas that will help the population accept some of the things that are being received by those of you who are beginning to understand new ways of co-creation.

Conservation of energies will be turned inward upon the solar system, and, therefore, you will understand new ways of generating energy for the planet by use of the natural forces being beamed into the planet according to the laws of the universe.

Combinations of light waves will be captured by new machines which can be entered into the programming of the Life Force in quickening the agent of fruition within the idea of survival methods of remembrance. Let not your hearts be troubled about these words, for they will soon be quickened in the scientific minds of many of you upon the earth. In other words, there will come a time when many of you will be harnessing new understandings coming from a realm of depth of the Father/Mother's house that has been programmed to help the earth begin anew.

Again, the way to the alignment and the attunement of these new ideas is through the chambers of the heart--deep silence, rest, devotion, and surrender of all of the ideas that have accumulated as the current reality of the mind.

Programming from an inner level has been authorized from on High now in the minds and the hearts of the devoted of the Lord. The programming has been quickened now for those of you who are ready for assignments that have aligned with your hearts desire. Trust that what you feel on inner levels of being is what is coming through to you from the Shekinah love of God. Be assured that what is given to you for emancipation is coming to the heart chakra and then moving into the realm of wisdom.

As wisdom unfolds into the conscious mind, and it is

held with a devotion to the almighty I AM for its induction, then that which has been programmed and written in your heart will come into manifestation, and you will be guided into the realm of the place on the earth where you need to serve the most.

Many adjustments will take place in the minds and hearts of those who are being quickened into the service that is written in your heart. You must be willing to go through these adjustments, and they are such a fine tuning method that you will be quickened in every way, and you will feel energy impulses that are very strange in your mental, your emotional and your physical bodies.

As these adjustments are being made, you may begin to feel as though you are losing a lot of yourself. That is exactly what is happening. The self that you have known in the past is diminishing in size, and the Self of God is making Itself known into the awareness of your crown chakra.

The crown chakra is the throne upon which the Christ must sit in order to make all things brand new. From this point of vision, the Christ can see all of the Kingdom of God within you as the programmed reality of your being. And as the Christ puts forth the spoken word within the consciousness of yourself, the spoken word then goes forth and returns into the being and the experience for which it is spoken and revered.

Understand that this point of awareness, within the

crown where Christ resides, is the temple of God that is referred to in the many scriptures, and this is the point of assignment from which the Christ within must dictate to the rest of this earthly self.

You become the servant and take all of the dictates of the King within the Temple and follow through on every command. Only in this way can there be divine order in the relinquishment of the old ways and the bringing forth, into the Kingdom of the cellular structure of the self, that which is written in the heart of each of you.

Perhaps some of you have been questioning the ways that things are going in your own particular incarnation and the many chaotic experiences of life that you are experiencing in such quantum proportions. Rest assured this is the result of the prayer of your heart to be used by the Spirit in this world to help make a better place. Everything that is not conducive to the participation of this bringing forth in the earth must be transmuted by the King who sits upon the throne in the crown. And everything that is not of love and light and compassion must be brought into love and light and compassion.

As these things are brought into these energy fields, there is often resistance. The resistance then creates the chaotic understanding of the conscious mind which does not comprehend the relationship between love and light and peace and joy, and the relationship that seems to be going on in the earth.

Many of you will begin to question what is sane and what is not, and if all of you is there. Trust that all of you is always there, but the part of you that feels separated is now falling into alignment with the all of you that is always there. In this falling, there is often fear of letting go. This is the hardest part for the mental mind to unclasp. Attachments to the separated experience have accumulated such a stronghold in the heart that it is difficult for the heart to be wrenched loose in letting go. At this point, it is imperative that you call upon the Holy Spirit to help you relinquish your attachments.

All suffering is the result of attachments in the heart. The nature of who you are cannot survive with the understanding and the energy that attachments create in the consciousness, for attachment is not a part of the living, loving, all free flowing God Almighty. There is such a free flow of giving in God that this must all be brought into the free flow.

Every day, it is imperative that you practice non-attachment to all things -- to your life even, for it is of God. Let go of your relationships, and, therefore, enable one another to breathe. Let go of the need for things, and the things will be filled to capacity. Let go of your attachments to everything that elevates the sense of separation. These will be multied and varied. It behooves you, Dear One, to make a list of that for which you think you have a need.

Let go of every cry for mercy to the Lord God, for mercy is the gift of love. Crying will not bring more of this mercy into your life, only an open palm in your heart will do so. Rest in the openness of receptivity, for mercy is already the gift of love within you. Open every cell with your word of openness. Open every cell. Open every cell. Instruct every cell to open to the blessings of the Almighty, for they simply await an acceptance. There is nothing more to be given.

Beloved angels of the Almighty God are assisting you now. They come as light and joy and peace, and they rest upon the shoulders of the true Self. Messengers from God is the accurate representation of these Light Beings. Compassion and generosity is the nature of their givingness. With joy and light and love they serve. Glorifying God in service of compassion is their mission. Remember Beloved, you are created only a little less than the angels.

You are really elevating now as you move into an open mind and heart of receptivity to the angel within you. So, do not be surprised if you feel your wings spreading in the earth and you are taking flight in the morning. You are being elevated to the angel consciousness within you.

Forever in the mind of God is the eternal reality of Itself. As this eternal reality awakens within the created, the majesty of the Kingdom of God corresponds to the frequency of the majesty within the Kingdom on earth. The beauty that shall be experienced by the awakened eye of love at the center of the heart is beyond compare.

The earth will begin to release a color vibration that has yet to be attuned to with the human eye. The vividness of every color of every created thing will begin to be known by those of you who have the inner eye of God opened. You will see as the all-seeing, all-knowing, all-loving, all-peaceful eye of God as it roves across the globe, viewing Its own creation. How many of you now are beginning to awaken to this new color frequency?

Precious moments in God's house will begin to become a common experience among you. The door of the Kingdom is opening wide, and many of you are entering at this time into an awareness of love that has never before been experienced by you. As this door opens, many of the companions of your Self will enter there with you. Here there will be a wonderful party of love, joy and praise given to the Almighty One.

It is important for you to celebrate this joy in the earth's experience. As you begin to celebrate the joy of the Lord in the earth, many more of the rooms will open from within, revealing to you even more to be joyful about and to celebrate.

Precious Ones, be assured that, as God continues to reveal Itself in the earth, you will continue to reveal yourself in many dimensions of expression. So much is left yet to be revealed. You have only just begun to understand the true

Self and the multiple expressions of who you are and why you are created.

Your evolution of light continues forever. This is eternal life, and, as the eternal life within you continues in the eternal now to express itself, the multitude of ways and expressions of yourself become as unlimited as eternal life itself. Nothing that you understand now will seem important to you in the New Age upon the earth. Everything that you understand will have expanded to such a degree that it will all seem new.

Fortunately, we are moving in a time-space continuum that has no marked value in accordance with the time-space continuum of old. Any time that the earth spins one more frequency of vibration in addition to that for which it has been spinning, the time continuum increases to the velocity in earth. Correlations of time, spinning from many galaxies, are incorporating their energies to help the New Earth birth itself into the light of love.

Consciousness turned in upon itself creates a spinning similar to that of which I am speaking. Actually, it is this turning within that is increasing the velocity of the earth in its own spinning, thus creating the possibility for a New Heaven and a New Earth.

Imperative in the New Birth is the process known as prayer and meditation. This I have emphasized in previous chapters. Rest assured that this is one of the most important components necessary for the increased velocity of the mind that will be needed to bring forth the new love.

People will begin to love one another as Christ loves them. This will become an innate opportunity, not a practiced one. But practice is what quickens the innateness of the capacity to love one another. Practice the presence of love. Love, love, love! Every time you feel an urge from the human self to judge one another, cancel it with the tendency to move forward, to reach out and to love.

Recognize that any need to judge is not a need to judge at all, but to love. Judgement is a frequency of separateness. It does not exist in the mind of Christ. This does not indicate that you will not make decisions ... wise ones, but you will not condemn or release the elixir of judgement upon one another, for to do so is to degenerate and tear down the frequency of the regenerating eternal Life Force. This delays the progress and the compassion that is being born in the earth. Do not do it, Beloved! Any time that you release any kind of restrictive or constrictive energy such as judgement, or hate, or resentment or anger, this increases the sense of separation and makes your progress slow.

You are not to understand now all of the ramifications of allowing this type of energy to be released from your heart. If I were to tell you all that this could possibly create, it would astound you into such shame as to bring you into a feeling of remorse and guilt, and that is not my purpose. The purpose for this statement is to help you understand the imperative need for love in the earth. Whatever you must do to compel yourself into loving ... do it! Most of all, call upon the indwelling Love that you are to love through you.

Very often it is difficult for the human mind, which is so captured in the sense of separation, to bring forth the energy of the inner Self. Therefore, offer the inner Self the opportunity to come forth and to do it for you. This is the way and the purpose of your existence in the earth at this time. You must conquer the separated self and bring it into the reality of union.

Presently there will appear for many of you a loving Presence of guidance. Some of you will feel this Presence of guidance as though it is something separate from yourself. It is not! The reason that it may feel as though it is separate from yourself is that you have separated yourself from it for so long it feels like a new friend to you. Jesus referred to this when He said, "I have called you friend." The friend of Christ has been among your acquaintance forever, but, for some reason unknown to you, now it is coming forth in its full friendship and will continue to deepen as you continue to communicate and to be with this friend. The day will come when you will recognize this friend as yourself and know, beyond a shadow of a doubt, that you have been in holy relationship from the beginning. Beloved Angels of the Light, rest now in the remembrance of this holy relationship.

CHAPTER 10

WINGS OF SPIRIT

Rest in the assurance that the love of God is the continuum upon which the planet is now functioning. Every aspect of the planetary circle of human beings is now being brought into the light of this eternal love.

Soon there will be placed upon this planet the Merkabah realization of I AM. Into this frequency of light there will be sent into you a beautiful White Dove resting at the center of your heart as the symbol of the Eternal One returning into the earth. This symbol is not just a symbol, but it is the actual Presence of the Winged One within you. Be assured that this symbol is there, placed in the heart of the child of God and knowing what it is supposed to accomplish in the earth.

It has been known for many aeons of time by the ancient ones that symbols actually exist in the realm of Divine Mind as implementations of the divine idea for which they stand. As these symbols enter into the heart remembrance of the child of God, they help to quicken that state of awareness within.

The Great White Dove of Peace has been known in

earth for many, many years as that which is lifted as part of the plan for peace. As the Great White Dove expands in the awareness of the consciousness of the individual, the promise of the return of life at a frequency vibration higher than that which is known to humankind at this point will begin to manifest itself in the earth. This is the promise of the love of God within the heart of each child.

The Dove of Peace is the symbol of the Life Force that rises above the earth consciousness of the human being as it is known now. Resting in the assurance that this is the heart of God opened to its fullest capacity of beingness, you can understand then that all is in divine order according to the Will and the work of the Holy One.

Listen to the heart chakra as the Winged Dove begins to expand and lift you into understandings of mental, emotional and physical levels that correspond to the Jesus Christ understanding as He walked in the earth.

The man from Nazareth was a being of light that came from above. When Jesus spoke of this "above," He was not speaking of a home somewhere on another planet or another place in God. He was speaking from the consciousness of the Winged Dove that had baptized Him in the Jordan.

The Dove is, again, the symbol of the Holy Spirit of God moving in you to capture that which has been lost in the consciousness of humanity. Baptism is a sign that the Holy

Spirit is lifting you out of the earth into the above in awareness.

At the beginning of the ministry of Jesus Christ it was the Winged Dove that carried Him above the earth and made it possible for Him to claim, "I AM from above, you are from below." In the below state of mind, the human being has difficulty understanding the relationship between God and the human being. As the Winged Dove lifts you above the consciousness of that which you think you are, you will begin to lose the remembrance of that which was below. As this remembrance is lost, or perhaps more accurately stated transmuted into the truth, you will be set free in Christ Jesus.

If you will come into the awareness that I AM is birthing you and lifting you, then you will know that the descent of the Dove is upon you in great proportions of gracefulness.

The Star of David is also a precious symbol that is being placed in the hearts of the awareness of humankind. This is the symbol of the ascending mind of the human being and the descending consciousness of the spiritual human being, merging and bringing into union the two which are one.

Pressure is not of this point in time. Pressure comes as the descent of the Dove increases the velocity of the energy that is from above. Thus is the spiritual transformation. Pressure in the soul erupts in many ways as the human being is lifted above the earth consciousness. For some of you it feels as though you have been scattered. Confusion and loss of the old self feels like a pressure from the inside out, bursting forth something within you that is unfamiliar. For some of you, this pressure from above is understood as a quickening of the Life Force at the very center of the physical body that cannot be detected by any medical profession. This is the Life Force known in the scriptures as eternal life, which is the energy that brings down the Spirit merging it with all of the human being.

As the Spirit lifts the body into the love vibration, pressure is often felt in the mental, the emotional and the physical self. Again, this pressure will be perceived by each one of you differently. According to that which needs to be lifted, it is guided from above by God.

To assure the least amount of discomfort in the lifting of the physical to the spiritual awareness, it is encouraged of the little children to come as child into the heart chamber and rest with open minded acceptance and surrendered mind and heart, reaching out and up to the spiritual Self for the lifting.

You have been brought to a certain mind understanding according to the intellect. This has been absolutely necessary in developing within you the conscious awareness of co-creation. The point of awareness at which you now rest in the mind is conducive for the control necessary for surrender to the Divine. Lift up your mind and heart now, controlled by the illumined intellect to a degree and intensity of total surrender to the Spirit. Do not be afraid to offer all of your awareness to the Spirit. This is the frequency of surrender necessary in order to be lifted above the earth consciousness into the spiritual awareness.

As the decent of the Dove lifts the human into the spiritual human, you will begin to feel the pressure of life's misconceptions being lifted as if there is a time of total human transformation taking place within your body structure. Again, I offer to you the possibility that this is not a time of extreme comfort for the human being, but it is one that is necessary if you are to embark and give birth upon the earth to a new love.

It is written in the hearts of all of the children of God that this new love must come forth as part of the Divine Plan for the fulfillment of eternal life in the human being. Your body structures will thus begin to change as the pressure of the Life Force lifts each cellular memory into what is known by you now as light body consciousness.

Go forth now into your time of transformation with great joy, and as pressure comes upon the mental, the physical, the emotional body self, do not be alarmed in any way, for this is the gift of God's Grace. The Dove of Peace is finding a conscious home within your soul. Such was the Dove of Peace that descended into the being of Jesus Christ that enabled Him to weather the storms of the tribulation that always will be in the earth until all of humanity is lifted to the point of peace in the heart of God.

Truly, there are among you many Light Beings now who have been quickened by the spiritual Self. It is obvious as you look into the media that the life of God is penetrating into every aspect of earth's experience. The love of God has penetrated the veils of separation to the point that the focus of humanity is turning to the Self in every area of experience. As this awareness continues to penetrate into the manifest world of experience, it will help to lift the frequency of love in every expression of life.

Presently, in the place of the traumatic experiences of life and death, will come into being in your media experiences of eternal life. Welcome these new experiences of eternal life, and identify your awareness with this principle of reality. Let go of the concept of death as has been introduced into the experience of humankind. This type of suffering has simply resulted again from that continual mind awareness of separation. As the Dove lifts the consciousness into the realization of union, the eternal life idea will begin to impregnate itself more and more in the earth's experience in every way. Begin to look to the media of communications for this eternal life message, and identify with it as your own.

Written in the hearts of the children of God is a message of great importance. The importance is the fulfillment of the Divine Plan from God. Every planetary system that is created by God has a unique purpose. Earth's purpose is for the enlightenment of the consciousness of being that is being brought into this new framework.

The Dove of Peace is the importance that is being birthed; for this peaceful state of consciousness, added to the dimensions of consciousness already created in the universe, is a balancing factor that is necessary for the entire cosmos to function in divine order.

Peace on earth, good will to all, is the message of the importance. As love breaks forth on the Winged Dove, peace is the center of that lifting. Continue to entertain the words, "Peace, be still." If you will, remember that the message Jesus returned to the disciples was, "Peace I leave with you; my peace I give to you; not as the world gives do I give to you." The Christ within is the peaceful Dove of love, and this is the gift of the union that is taking place. Rest in the assurance that the peace of God is the gift of Grace and the importance of earth's gift to the universe.

Each of you has tapped into the peace of the Great White Dove at times and knows the unspoken gift that cannot be expressed as you rest in this state of awareness. This is to become the eternal life quality of the soul of each human being. It serves as the receptacle for the divine ideas presented to the individual consciousness from God. This receptacle of consciousness within you is birthed, then, to the divine ideas of co-creation that God would have implemented through your individualization of Itself.

Make me an instrument, Lord, of Thy peace. Hold this thought in your mind. Such a prayer is impulsed from on High. Finding resonance in your heart, it thus is lifted up on the wings of the Dove and will become the eternal reality of your awareness. This is the beginning of conscious co-creation, the energy necessary to implement the Divine Plan in the earth.

The God Almighty is a most precious God. Sweet Holy Spirit is the emissary of this preciousness. "Sweet Holy Spirit. Sweet heavenly Dove. Stay right here with us, filling us with your love." Is that not a song that is sung among many of you these days?

The Dove of sweet Holy Spirit is the precious gift of God sweeping the earth's consciousness into the cleanliness and purity of heart that was described by Jesus, which is necessary if you are to see God in expression.

"Blessed are the pure in heart, for they shall see God." Remember this quote from the Master teacher. It is the sweet Holy Spirit that is helping to purify the heart so that the love vibration can be released from the center of peace.

In this purification process, many of you will escape some of the pressure that has been filling the hearts, souls, and bodies of other children in the earth. The human mind cannot capture the reasoning why some are experiencing more pressure than others. But understand that it has to do with God's Grace at work according to the consciousness frequency of the Light Bearers who are now penetrating the earth's atmosphere with the vibration of love and peace in alignment with the Divine Plan.

Many of you are on assignments that you cannot remember, and thus you are carrying into the earth your gift of love in many individual ways. Pressure for one is not pressure for another. Pressure for one is often pressure for another.

Healing and lifting through the activity of the Holy Spirit is not an individual thing because you are not separated. As one is lifted on the wings of the Holy Spirit, because of the reality of your oneness, others are lifted with you. Was it not, again, the Master who referred to the great truth; when I AM lifted up, I draw all men unto me?

Do not compare your lifting with another, for the point upon which you stand in the earth is completely different from the point at which your brother and sister stand. Each individual child of God has established in consciousness an awareness that is peculiar to each individual, and the lifting of the Dove is the only awareness that knows what is necessary for each one. This is the gift of God's Grace; again, the sweet Holy Spirit, sweet heavenly Dove.

You are in the very midst of a time that is extremely important in the earth. As you come together realizing your unity and oneness, it will be a great time in the earth of celebration. It is important for you to gather together in this celebration and in this transformation. As your mental, emotional and physical selves gather in small rings of love, there is a great network of ringed beingness that is created and spread around the earth. These rings serve as simple reminders of the eternal life circle that has no beginning and no end.

I encourage you to form in small circles for prayer and meditation serving as a wedding ring upon the finger of God. Each circle will help to bring about the mystical marriage within the individual soul and, collectively you will come into rings of empowerment and enlightenment, serving in the earth and becoming a part of the collective eternal circle of love and light which is symbolic of the way in which the globe is formed.

With bowed heads in prayer, the energy of love is descended from above. The above is within you, not without. As the descent occurs, you will feel lifted up from the earth into a tremendous energy of peace. It will pass all understanding with the mind and simply must be experienced in order to be comprehended.

Come together in circles of love with bowed heads and opened hearts. Ask for the descent of the holy Dove to be a part of the circle's experience. Collective prayer generates a frequency of energy that is not understood by you now...the One in the many, and the many in the One. You will be lifted, and you will begin to heal the veils of separation in quantum proportions as you gather in the name of Jesus Christ. Again, I encourage you to bow your heads .... a symbol of release of the intellect ... and lift your hearts in openness.

Become as little children in your circles of prayer. By this I encourage you to move into spontaneity and not structure. Let each experience of prayer take on a life of its own. Do not be focused on certain patterns of prayer, but come together in sweet surrender, allowing the Holy Spirit to dictate the form in which the structure will be implemented.

Each experience will probably be different for each of you and for each collective group; for the ways of the Spirit are not known to the ways of the human mind, and, thus, you must come as a little child ... open, receptive, accepting, innocent, waiting, trusting in God's Winged One to lift you into the experience that only the Winged One can.

Each time your prayer groups meet, there will be a consciousness raising that may not be tangible at first, but as you continue to devote yourself to the pranamed position of surrender, you will begin to experience an incredible infusion of love. You will be gathered together with greater intensity and frequency, desiring to be used by the Spirit as part of the divine healing for Mother Earth. As the prayer for use is born in your heart, continue to offer it up. This again is part of the

Divine Plan. You are being made into the instrument of peace through which the love of God can pour forth to help lift the entire human race.

CHAPTER 11

THROUGH THE ARCHES

It is written in the hearts of the children of God, the love, the peace and the power that is so sought after in the earth has to be expressed from an inner level of awareness. Love, peace and power cannot be captured in the outer experience of earth before it is released from an inward understanding.

As we move into this new time in the earth's experience, so many new teachings will be expressed. It will be difficult for many of you to recognize that God's Will is always in a constant changing modality, and yet the Spirit of God is a constant that never changes. The creative principle is always bringing forth experiences of newness. Sometimes, resistance to the change is not comfortable. It makes one move in circles of incompatibility.

It is imperative that the children of God open themselves now to the creativeness of Spirit and to the inner wisdom that is revealed in openness. Just as when a room goes dark when the light is shut out, and there is nothing going on, such it is as the door shuts upon the chambers of wisdom in the heart. Open the door of wisdom. Open the door of experience. Open the door of restingness. Open the door of all there is to be received in God's house.

The way the door is opened is very simple. Consent to the creative love and wisdom of the Holy Spirit and bring to earth's experience an open mind and heart. Be willing to let go of every preconceived notion of reality and come into a greater awareness of the Holy Spirit's workings.

Rise above the temptations to allow your mind and heart to be trapped in a circle of continuous remembrance of old. If you stay trapped in a continuous remembrance of old, the new reflects the same remembrance. God is not sameness. God is constant creative wonder.

The love of God penetrates into the chambers of remembrance. When this takes place in the beloved child, the Holy Spirit is thus enabled to quicken a new remembrance in accordance with Divine Will. The Will of God penetrates into the awareness and, through the constant appearance of love in the memory, creates a new heaven and a New Earth in the child.

Presently, there will come a peace in the world that will erupt all un-peace. Just as the light coming in the darkness dispels all darkness, so will peace coming into the world dispel all un-peace. As this peace is being born from the hearts of the children, it will be very important for each one of you to enter through the archway of the peaceful Presence awaiting at the center of your heart.

Coming into this archway is a guided tour from the inner Self. It is important for you to have a spiritual guide, for the lost child doesn't know the way. You are being guided even now as you read these words. Guidance appears in the moment, according to what you are experiencing. As you continue to open to the possibility of an inner guide, then this guide can come forth to assist you through the doorway. The inner guide is the Holy Spirit, the teacher ... remember? And I will send you an inner teacher, an inner counselor, an inner guide, an inner presence, a companion of love. The guide is the Spirit of you. It is who you really are, bringing to your conscious memory a mystical marriage of this truth.

The archway is the entrance into God's remembrance, the home of the Eternal One. It is the doorway. It is the power of communion appearing as a symbol. Let not your heart be filled with doubt, as this keeps the door shut. It is not important for you to understand what is beyond the doorway in your current state of awareness. It would not make much sense then to enter through the doorway -- to see and experience the inner rooms -- if it was already your conscious reality, but since this is not the case, it is important that you surrender the path to the Holy Spirit and allow this precious Presence to guide your every step as you approach the archway of God's Kingdom.

Before too many years pass in the earth, it will be recognized by the children of God the great wonder and majesty of God. Such recognition ignites within the heart the elixir of joy as never before yet experienced by the child. As this elixir of joy erupts and becomes the energy functioning from the center of peace, the entire cosmos will be blessed by the collective bubbles of happiness rising out of the earth's plane of existence.

I remind you all once again, that you are not earthbound. Extend your energy to the farthest star and beyond. Everything is affected. You are a ripple of love. It moves from your center point of peace, out upon the waves of eternal life, and it registers in that which exists. Allow this joy and peace and love to draw you into the center of Itself, thus bringing to your remembrance that which is true in your God Self.

The wisdom of God has no remembrance of ignorance. You are immersed in wisdom. Present to the energy of prayer the heart's desire for wisdom to become more of the conscious experience. As your prayer is lifted, so will the wisdom be lifted in you. It was our friend, Solomon, who understood the "open sesame" of the prayer of wisdom. The beginning of wisdom is to pray for wisdom, and, as God releases Itself as wisdom, the joy in the heart will be lifted to such an intensity of thanksgiving that it will become a magnetic attracting force for greater wisdom.

Wisdom frees the soul and lifts it out of bondage. In earth, you have experienced what is known as much ignorance of reality. Wisdom is the medical healing Presence of God that makes adjustments according to the natural way of life. When we are out of sync with wisdom, much confusion erupts in manifestation. Uncertainty becomes an experience of extreme horror for the individual. Outer experiences seem to come together and crash into one another. It feels as though there is no such thing as Divine Order. Such is the consciousness which needs a shot of wisdom.

In the earth there are many points in manifestation that are now reflecting a need for a transfusion of wisdom. Enter into the chambers of the heart. This is the place where the archway to the door of wisdom resides. Love is all there is. It is God. The heart chamber is the archway through which love expresses itself in all of its properties. Entering through this chamber enables you to stretch forth your hand and partake of the Tree of the Knowledge of Wisdom. Love and wisdom united in holy wedlock become the magnetic force for co-creation.

In the beginning you were sent out from God's awareness of union. The union in God was not a conscious reality, but an experiential reality of union. In the expulsion of you into manifest reality, the union that was known at the beginning was lost. It was important for this loss to take place. It would be impossible for you to remember and become conscious co-creators if this particular experience of expulsion had not taken place. That is about as simple as I can make it. Therefore, it is important that you release all sense of guilt about leaving God's house. This was not an activity of your conscious willfulness, but an impulse from God as a part of the Divine Plan of co-creation.

The Life Force is innocent. Compelled by an inner impulse to co-create, you thus entered into a manifest state, increasing in complexity as wisdom and love impulsed you onward, inward, upward, outward ... stretching you beyond realities previously known in each moment. Even now, you are continuing to be stretched by love and wisdom. You are becoming boundless ... boundless ... boundless! Infinite possibilities await the stretch of each new moment. Do not resist the stretch.

As in your educational movements, each day in the classroom gives forth the opportunity to be stretched. Wisdom is the focus of the educational system, as it is understood that wisdom creates an individual that is creative and productive in the earth. All that is now studied in the educational systems has come forth as the result of consciousness being penetrated by the infinite wisdom of God. Therefore, beloved Angels of the Light, enter into the chambers of your heart through the archway of the door of wisdom, and here you will be the author for the new text for the new educational system. There is no limit to the wisdom that is yet to be revealed in the earth. Actually, wisdom has only just begun.

It is important for you to understand that residing within you is a child with an I.Q. beyond compare. It is also important for you to understand that, just as the child grows naturally from an infant to an adult in size, you are literally being grown from within. You have no control over this growth. It is omniscience, the intelligence of God, that is growing you. What is it that makes the child stretch in size from infant to adult? Could it be anything other than the wisdom of God? Very much like this simple explanation, the child within you, which is wisdom itself, is being stretched into adulthood. This stretching is the Will and the work at the impulse of the wisdom of Spirit.

There is an infinite wisdom in Spirit that knows all and knows how to do the Will and the work of the Almighty God in the child. Can you not see then how important it is for you to relax in your growth and not be anxious about anything in the earth. Does the child express anxiety as it is moving from birthday to birthday? The child rejoices and is excited standing before the mirror to see if it is any taller than it was yesterday. And, over time of course, it is obvious, as your photographs capture, that the stretch has taken place, and the child knows not how it happened. Such is what is going on in comparison within the soul of the children of God in the earth.

Each day in the earth is a birthday for you, an

opportunity for you to stand before the mirror of yourself and observe the incomparable wisdom of God at work. Such wisdom! Such wisdom! The reasoning mind questions how you can be growing at such a rapid rate and changing before your very eyes. It would be impossible for your reasoning mind to capture what is going on. God is wisdom. You are the effect of wisdom.

Beyond your wildest imaginings, it is written in your heart that which will come forth. You will soon be entering into an awareness of yourself that will even astound your wildest dreams. The human potential for co-creation is truly in an infant stage at the moment. However, your birthday is right around the corner. Each one of you has been endowed with special gifts as part of the Divine Plan for the co-creation. The birth of the wisdom and the love of God will reveal these gifts. As these gifts are unwrapped through the stretching of the intelligence within you, many of you will be surprised as to the way and the what of the gift within you.

There are clues to help you realize what the gifts of love and wisdom may be. So simple are the clues and easy to find, and yet to some it seems as though they are hidden. "What is my special gift to the world," you may ask? Ask yourself the question, "When have I been the happiest?" This question will reveal to you a portion of your gift. That which makes the child the happiest is a clue that what is written in your heart will create in you that same joy when opened to full view, and that is why the psalmist has said to enter into the joy of the Lord. Call forth all activities that generate this happiness and joy, and immerse yourself in participation. As you continue to immerse yourself in the participation of joy, the gift of your specialness will be revealed, and that inner omniscient guide will draw you into the place of givingness where you can give what you love to do the most.

Paradise is giving from your special gifts. As you give the gift that is written in your heart, a fountain of youth will begin to spring forth at the very center of all life within you. You are an eternal being awakening to the reality of the gifts of love and wisdom within you. These gifts that you are bringing into manifestation are part of the wisdom understanding that will help you know why you were created.

Each of you was created with purpose in God mind. None of you is without purpose. If you do not know your purpose, that does not dispute the reality that purpose is written in your heart. There is an omniscient Divine Plan at the center of all creation, and each manifestation of creation is important to the whole. You are important to the whole. Without you, there is no whole. Do you understand this at all? Contemplate it deeply. It is important. You are important! You ... are ... important!

CHAPTER 12

HOLY RELATIONSHIPS

Jesus Christ is the oversoul for planet earth. His love and light are guiding each of you into the path that is right for you. As you continue in His word, His word will continue in you. Rest assured that His love and His presence is the guiding light at the center of your way. Jesus Christ is drawing you into the realm of your own Christ so that, together, you can continue in the co-creative plan of Father/Mother God. Rest in the assurance that Jesus Christ goes before you and directs your path.

Jesus Christ is the Son of God, and you, too, are the beloved Son. Your union and oneness in God enables Jesus Christ to make Himself known in you.

You are entering into a time in which the awareness of Jesus Christ will become the center point of awareness for the race mind. This is union in God, and it is the consciousness being established in the earth.

The love of God that Jesus Christ exemplified as He walked the earth in physical form is the exact duplicate of the consciousness that will walk in each of you. Collectively, as this awareness awakens, miracles will begin to happen around the globe in quantum proportions. Healings will begin to take place instantaneously. Many of you will actually have visitations from the Master. So many miraculous things will begin to happen. This will be the beginning of the new age known as the New Jerusalem.

An entire globe known as New Jerusalem will create a universal pattern of wholeness. Each one of you is a contributor to the wholeness, and you are being lifted and programmed for your particular importance in the plan. Every time you come into a greater awareness of this divine potential, the illumination of Jesus Christ rests more deeply in your soul. Every time you rest more deeply in the soul of Jesus Christ, you will become more aware of the importance of your particular identity.

Jesus Christ considers earth His incarnate home. It was here that it was made possible for Him to become the oversoul of the earth. The energy upon this planet is a particular graceful expression of God's drawingness into Itself. This is the purpose of planet earth...a place where possibilities can come into the fullness of expression. Look through eyes of conscious awareness and understand that each experience is a part of the graceful draw to fulfillment.

Look to each other as messengers from God, releasing and expressing importance for each other. In your journey back into God's home, each person that makes an appearance in your life is of great importance. The coming together of the two of you creates an energy pattern that explodes the possibility of fulfillment. Always meet each encounter with an awareness that it is a Holy one--a divine appointment on the journey.

Rest assured that Jesus Christ is at the center of the union of every relationship, drawing you together in His name. As you come together with conscious awareness of the Holy encounter, empty your mind and heart of preconceived expectations, allowing the holiness to fill the moment. In this realization, you will become more attuned to the Grace that is being exchanged between you.

The Lord your God at the center of your beingness is seeking to express Itself in greater fullness in the earth. Rest assured that each encounter is a revelation of who YOU are, looking through YOUR eyes. Because of the reality of union, each of you reflects to the other the perfect pattern of wholeness at your center. Sometimes the reflection does not appear to be perfect, and thus you have the reflection of the journey, a return journey into conscious reality.

The heartbeat of each of you is the heartbeat of God. Be not afraid to understand the unity of the heartbeat. As your heart beats with conscious awareness of union, each encounter will become an exciting adventure. You must learn to listen to your heart for the message that comes to you with each acquaintance. The message that is spoken in relationship is a powerful one for healing and transformation. Holy relationships are catalysts for the eruption of the Christ in manifestation.

The Presence of Jesus Christ at the center of each encounter is assured. Jesus Christ is the principle of the Son of God, and there is no place on the earth where you can find yourself that this principle is not active. If two of you in the earth come together agreeing in relationship for birthing of the truth, it shall be accomplished in His name.

Trust that each time you ask God to be lifted into the awareness of Jesus Christ, whatever presents itself in your earth experience is a gift of love impulsing you toward that awareness. Know that Jesus Christ, your brother, walks beside you in this journey.

Look not with the eyes of the mind at the encounter's blessings, but with the eyes and the ears of the heart. Absorb the graceful impulse drawing you into love. Trust that what you hear is always drawing you nearer to God. If you will trust this method, you will soon begin to actually see the love of God working in every situation to bring you to a greater realization of your very own divinity in Christ Jesus.

Every encounter is a Holy relationship, a divine appointment of Grace. Some of you will be moving into relationships of a longer duration. Many of you have been separated in lifetimes past, and these separations have left scars in the heart. Be not surprised now as you re-encounter one another and love becomes the healing balm to remove the scars of the soul that have not measured to the Jesus Christ divinity in each of you.

As you call forth your own love potential, you will serve in the relationship as the mystical healer. Forget that which you have not agreed upon in the past, and look to that truth that now resides within you both as the only reality between you.

The ever loving, everlasting God reveals Itself in you. Look in the mirror of each other's eyes, allowing permission for passage all the way to the heart. As you do this, the eyes of God centered at the heart of each of you will begin to see the perfection in one another. Conscious awareness of the purity and perfection of each of you becomes a catalyst for the drawing forth of this truth into the world of manifestation.

The power of love to unite is incomprehensible. The power to heal is beyond understanding. The power of love is the power of God. You are the love of God expressing, and you are fully endowed with all that the power can possibly express.

Surrender yourself to this preciousness of yourself and allow it to take full control. As you do this, and as you walk in the earth's journey home, you will begin to truly understand how much your God adores you. You are loved beyond your capacity to understand at this time, but, as you continue to accept the possibility that you are the love of God expressing, this reality will dawn in every aspect of your being and will reveal to you the great truths of love itself.

Thus, you truly begin to walk in the footsteps of the Master, Jesus Christ, becoming your very own Master in the earth. This is to follow Him. Follow Him into the regeneration. Follow Him into the overcoming. Follow Him into the ascension.

The children of God are gathered. There are no coincidences in the Gathering of Light. Every encounter is a precious moment and an opportunity to love. Every act of service is a conditioned response of the Jesus Christ principle functioning in the world to bring about the Divine Plan, and, Precious Ones, there is such a glorious Divine Plan written in your heart.

Do not question each encounter and relationship that is brought into your journey, but welcome it with open arms and open hearts, knowing that this is an opportunity for remembrance of the truth that will set you free. Be ever mindful of the moment in which you encounter one another. Stay present, recognizing the Presence and opening your heart to the gifts that you bring to one another. Focus on the gifts of love, the exchange of love between you. Focus only on the gifts.

It is written in your heart: you are the bringer of the gifts. Each one of you has a gift to share. Welcome each meeting as though it is a party of exchanging gifts, for that truly is what it is. Love one another in the exchange. Unite your minds and hearts becoming twin flames of Jesus Christ. Walk arm in arm, heart to heart. Listen with one heart for remembrance as God speaks to you through one another.

The presence and the power of God moving upon the face of Mother Earth is drawing forth a family which is bonding together as never before. You are each becoming conscious of the power that you carry in your hearts. Each one of you is becoming the brother and the sister relationship. Each one of you is creating in the earth a family of light connectedness that reaches around the globe in eternal life.

You should not look to the scriptures as rules and regulations that need to be followed in order to make this family unit possible, but as teachings of reality that you are inevitably being drawn into expressing. It is not that you should love one another. It is that you cannot help but do so as this family comes together in conscious awakening. The love that is being born in your heart now compels you into loving. It is the nature of your reality, and, thus, you must open yourselves to the flow of this river of love from within. It is not a presence and a power that can be learned, but only one that can be revealed in the learning.

Study the scripture with an open heart to this kind of understanding, and soon you will begin to read the words from the words themselves. Bring not your conscious mind to the pages of the truth. Bring your truth to the pages, and they will reveal to your conscious mind that which already is written in the pages of your own heart.

Sit with your Book of Life, allowing Jesus Christ, the oversoul of yourself, to turn the pages of remembrance, revealing to you that which is written. The story has already been authored. It is now simply being read into manifestation. It is a great experience and adventure. Enjoy it!

CHAPTER 13

ETERNAL LIFE IN CHRIST

Jesus Christ sends blessings to each one of you. His love and compassion is beyond the human mind's awareness, but you can feel this Presence in your heart.

You are now coming together as a powerful blessing of love into the cosmos of all createdness. Each one of us must understand the power and the Presence of immaculate conception. This is the birth of the individual soul which has experienced the mystical marriage with the inner Christ Presence. This takes place in the presence of love, for love is the frequency that brings forth the seed that unites with the fertile soil in the womb of the Spirit.

As love is born in the heart of the Beloved, a courtship of endearment brings the mind and the heart to the alter. As with any relationship, there are many opportunities for the purity of this love to express itself.

Continued in the relationship of devotion to one another, the love and the wisdom of the inner child creates a vortex of receptivity and open minded communion with the inner one known as God.

You are returning to the immaculate conception of

peace. The power of peace incorporates itself in the wisdom of God, and it brings forth this eternal union and remembrance of the quickened heart.

Sacrifice is imperative for this mystical marriage to take place. Coming from an understanding of true sacrifice, everything that is a possession of the heart must be offered to the presence of love. There can be no possessiveness in the mystical marriage union. All ideas of personal possession must be offered as the gift at the wedding feast. Therefore, Beloved, it is very important at this time that you collectively come to an understanding of that which you hold so tightly as being important in collective accumulation. Release these collective accumulations into a frequency of free flow, returning into God any idea of possession. Hold nothing with tenaciousness. Hold nothing in your heart against another human being. Hold nothing in your mind that is not selfless. Hold nothing in your life as though it were your very own.

The immaculate conception gives birth to the realization that all is God, and God is all. Nothing belongs to the created; all belongs to the Creator. Union is the result of total surrender to that which is being expressed through you as Creator.

It is important for you to move now into the temple of the altered Self and reside here in a constant presence of emptiness. Emptiness will provide the receptivity necessary for the mystical marriage to unite, and it will create within you a bond of union with the eternal flame of Jesus Christ. This is the twin flame of the soul which has yearned to find itself through aeons of incarnation in co-creation.

United in holy wedlock, the eternal flame of Jesus Christ gives birth to the child of love in the earth. This child of love brings forth a new beginning in the cycle of evolution into eternal life. As this birth takes place through the matrimonial commitment, the extension of the arm of God reaches into all manifestation.

Beloved Angels of Eternal Life, recognize that the union that is now taking place within you is the only one that will fulfill the longing in your heart for love. Each time you give yourself to this realization, you help yourself remember the immaculate conception.

The presence of love is drawing forth that which is contained within itself. You have been pregnant with love from the beginning, and the qualities of the soul being conceived in love have been developing over time. Much as the mother carries the child in the womb, allowing the entity to absorb the necessary components of humanity, so the seed of love impregnated within the womb of your heart has been nurtured by the original Source, Father/Mother God. As love is born in the earth, it is a companion to God.

Working together in the impulse of birth, realize that the birthing process is one of great joy. At the same time, there are the pains of giving birth to something new. That which has been growing in your heart is ready now to come forth in full manifestation in Mother Earth. It is important for you to cooperate with the birthing process and allow the impulse of love to push forth the new creature in Christ.

Little by little, you will descend through the canal of birth easing into full expression. Be not afraid as the push of love moves you forward though the canal. You may feel labor pains as love is coming forth in its fullness. This would be perceived by you as opportunities to stay focused in the reality of the birth of love in you. There is no return to a former state of being other than that which is now fully termed in you. You must give birth. You must!

Resting in the presence of love, you will begin to understand the empowerment of being a child of God. It is love that goes forth now from the new born child in you that co-creates a universe according to the original Divine Plan. It is love that goes before. It is love that carries you to that which has gone before. It is the power and the presence of love that brings forth the image and likeness of itself.

As you begin to walk in the earth as the Christ child, seeing for the first time the reality of love, the eyes through which you see will teach you. You will look nowhere else for your knowledge. Your heart will begin to listen to the instructions of God as you are carefully tutored and brought into fullness as an adult in Christ. The wisdom of God will teach you all things and bring to your remembrance that which was in the beginning immaculately conceived.

The promises of Jesus Christ are all written in your heart, now fulfilling the prophesy of old. Have no fear! The preordained destiny of mystical union is taking place within you this very moment.

Your consent to absorb the truth written in the pages of this expression of love has created within you the energy necessary for the fulfillment of that which was prophesied by Jesus Christ. This is the beginning. This is the Alpha of eternal life in Jesus Christ. There is no other way. There is no other reality. There is no other beginning. This is the New Earth. This is the new beginning. This is the new Book of Life.

Carry your will, now, in your heart, as you walk the earth as the child born in Christ. The will, carried in the heart, gathers all that is necessary for the continued unfoldment in Christ Jesus. The will, carried in the heart, becomes the impulse for the full realization of Christ in the soul. The greater assignments will then be revealed as you carry the will in the heart.

There are multiple layers of assignments that have yet to be revealed in the presence of love. As will is carried in the heart, these assignments grow to maturity and fulfillment. This is just the beginning of the New Age. There is so much more to be revealed to the Christ child.

The presence and the power of eternal life is the seed that is now carried in the genetic structure of the new born child. It is scattered with every thought and with every move to action in the earth, casting Its seeds among the many and the One. These seeds quicken a New Earth and bring forth the image and the likeness of the fruit that is innate within the seed.

Rest assured that the Son shall nourish that which is within the seed, drawing it into the fullest expression ... multiplied ... multiplied ... multiplied! Thus, we move into a new teaching in the earth: the Grace of the fathers is visited upon the children; the Grace of the mothers is visited upon the children; the Grace of God carries its seed into eternal life. Omni Ashni! Omni Ashni!

GLOSSARY OF TERMS

GLOSSARY OF TERMS

AEON:

Subcomponent of a consciousness time zone. Fundamental unit in the cycles of creation.

AGE OF ENLIGHTENMENT:

Time frame in the evolution of the consciousness of humanity related to the awakening to the reality of the nature of Being. Age now coming to an end.

AGE OF ASCENSION:

The next step in the evolution of humankind. Age known as the Christ. Age in which we will ascend in awareness and expression above the mind and into the realm of the known Presence of God. Age now upon us.

ALPHA:

The beginning. The starting point for a cycle of cosmic evolution.

ALPHA AND OMEGA:

Beginning and end of cycles of creation. All in all. Fragmented plurality and undifferentiated union. Symbolic of eternal divine nature of Christ.

ANGELS:

Messengers of God for hope. Created

from the compassionate heart of God to serve the Kingdom in a process known as joy. Angels assist in the awakening process through joy, and can be felt as a lifting power and a peace. They help to strengthen faith, for their energy rests in faith alone. Their healing capacity is an incredible graceful gift. "Be not afraid to ask for their assistance. It is their job."

ARC: A geometry of light wherein God's revelation is made known. A luminous bridge formed in a gap. A "spark."

ARK: Holy place, sanctuary, spiritual part of oneself -- Christ center within, original spark of divinity.

ASCENSION: Process of rising, lifting or being drawn into higher levels of awareness in and through the frequency of love. Unfoldment into spiritual wholeness.

ATTACHMENTS: Tenacious concepts of false belief giving rise to a "hold" on consciousness which restricts the divine idea of free flow in alignment with Grace. Attachments are the cause of all suffering.

BOOK OF LIFE: The story of the Divine Plan written in the heart of each, authored by the individualized I AM Presence. Book can only be read by resting at the center of the infinity of silence and allowing the seals of time's illusions to be broken. The book is opened by the yearning of the heart for God's Will to be done. As the book is opened, we are guided to that place of service that will enable us to become an important participant in the birth of the Christ Consciousness in the earth.

CATALYST: Something which provokes significant change. That which causes activity between forces without itself being affected.

CELESTIAL: Pertaining to Spirit or Divine.

CELLULAR MEMORY: Genetic blueprint in all of us.

CHAMBERED NAUTILUS: Spiral chambered shell, in this case representing the heart where the "still small voice" resides. Place where the archway to the door of Kingdom resides. The archway through which love expresses itself in all its properties. Entering through the chamber enables one to stretch forth and partake of the true knowledge of wisdom and the many mansion worlds.

CHILDREN OF GOD: All of us.

CHILDREN OF LIGHT: Children now coming into earth plane with a new understanding yet to be born in the earth. As these children enter into earth's atmosphere, they release the remembrance of who they are, thus quickening the adult population into remembrance. All beings who have been awakened in Christ consciousness.

CHRIST: The spiritual nucleus and true higher Self of every individual. The true light and guide within.

CHRIST HOME: Where the children of God birthing the Jesus Christ Consciousness reside.

CHRIST PRINCIPLE: Living principle working and abiding in each person as potential perfection. Divine inheritance of eternal life.

CO-CREATION:

Humanity's conscious co-participation with God in the implementation of the Divine Plan in the earth.

COLLECTIVE PRAYER:

Cumulative prayers of the Many in the One.

COMPASSION OF CHRIST:

A passion of love that is released into the service of all of the beings in the world. A passion for life itself reaching into the depths of the understanding heart. There is no understanding of separateness within this compassion which embraces the totality of every living thing on earth.

CONSCIOUSNESS:

From elementary perception to reflective thought - knowing that we know.

CROWN CHAKRA:

Where wisdom and spiritual understanding are centered at the top of the head. The throne upon which the Christ must sit in order to make all things new. From this point of vision, the Christ can see all of the Kingdom of God within as the programmed reality of being. Point of awareness, temple of God, and point of assignment from which Christ within dictates to the rest of the earthly self. The highest triad of Sephirothic Knowledge in human consciousness.

CRUCIFIXION: The giving up or crossing out of attachments. Surrender of the mortal to attain the immortal.

DARKNESS: Absence of Truth in consciousness. Seeming absence of light.

DIMENSIONS: Planes or realms of manifestation. Different levels of reality. Different states of consciousness.

DIVINE IDEA: The Christ Principle having encoded within it the structure and the elements for perfection. The Presence of God manifesting in human experience.

DIVINE MIND: The Father's thought form in the universe. God-Mind. Omnipresent, all-wise, all-loving, all-powerful Spirit.

DIVINE PLAN: The creative arrangement of life by God written in our heart.

DIVINE WILL:

The impulse of the eternal Life Force at the center of all createdness to fulfill itself. Divine Will is calling forth each person to health, abundance, joy, harmony, peace, wholeness and eternal life.

DOVE:

The symbol of the Holy Spirit moving in us to reveal that which has been lost in the consciousness of humanity.

ELOHIM:

Universal Principle of Divine Being behind veils of creation.

ENTROPY:

Collapse upon self. Negative decay, conversion or degeneration of matter-energy, as opposed to centropy -- electrification of matter-energy.

ETHERIC REALMS:

Spiritual, non-material realm in which we live, move and have our being, and out of which we create.

EYES:

The portal for passage into the heart. As we look into the mirror of each other's eyes, the eyes of God centered at the heart of each begins to see the perfection in one another. Conscious awareness of the purity and perfection of each becomes a catalyst for the drawing forth of this truth into the world of manifestation.

FATHER/MOTHER GOD'S
HOUSE: Christ consciousness fully realized in God.

FIGURE EIGHT: Symbol for infinity and the river of life swirling in every cell as the image and likeness of God. Meditation upon this symbol carries the secret of the mystery of the Kingdom within.

FORGIVENESS: The key to ascension resulting from forgetting the memory of separation and loneliness.

FREE WILL: The capacity to surrender and accept our destiny -- the inevitable choice for eternal life.

GATHERING OF LIGHT: Ingathering of those who choose to be chosen in service of the Light. A family of light connectedness reaching around the globe being brought together in a conscious awakening to eternal life and love. Ingathering of all sparks of Light into ecumenical Body or Community of Light. Light is equivalent to the love consciousness of Jesus Christ.

GOD:

Constant Creative Wonder and absolute good expressed in all creation. The one Presence and one power in the universe in whom we live, move, and have our being.

GOD'S WILL:

The impulse of love at the center of all action. When rested in at the center of the chambered nautilus within the heart, all goes in alignment with the Divine Will, and the way, and the truth and the life of Spirit.

GRACE:

That aspect of Divine Law that doesn't deal in even exchanging, but in the increase of good through greater giving. Divine assistance in the drawing forth remembered union in God. The principle of God's love at work in the fulfillment of the Divine Plan.

HEART:

An invisible center of consciousness through which love is received from Being. The archway through which love expresses itself in all of its properties.

HEART CHAKRA: Lit., "wheel," circle. The love center of vital energy in the human subtle body.

HOLY RELATIONSHIPS: Catalysts for the eruption of the Christ in manifestation. Jesus Christ is at the center of the union of every relationship. Each encounter is a Holy relationship, a divine appointment of Grace.

HOLY SPIRIT: Inner guide, counselor, teacher and presence. The infinite "breath" of God. The companion of love. Who we really are, bringing to our conscious memory a mystical marriage of this truth.

I AM PRESENCE: One's true identity, one's destiny. The Christ Mind of each individual. The indwelling Lord of life, love and wisdom. Expression "I AM THAT I AM" (in Hebrew "Ehyeh Asher Ehyeh") references "covenant" between human self and Christed Overself -- knowing of one's true identity, one's destiny. Holy salutation and mantra.

IMMACULATE CONCEPTION: "Seeding" of Divine Grace. The birth

of the individual soul which has experienced the mystical marriage with the inner Christ Presence. Love is the frequency that brings forth the seed that unites with the fertile soil in the womb of the Spirit giving birth to the realization that all is God, and God is all.

IMPULSE OF LOVE:

The most powerful transforming force in all of the universal systems of God's Kingdom. The uniting force that spins a web from universe to universe, unlocking many, many lifewaves joining us together in One. It draws us into full remembrance of the Divine Plan written in our heart.

INCREASING VELOCITY:

"He shortened the days." See Mark 13:20. "Speeding up" of consciousness time and intensification of spiritual love now being experienced.

INDWELLING PRESENCE:

Presence within man of Christ.

JESUS CHRIST:

Eternal Divine Son of the Father who incarnated as the Son of Man to lead us into eternal life. Oversoul for planet Earth -- the guiding light at the center "drawing" us into our own Christship.

JUDGMENT: Departure from law of love. Act of comparison or contrast based upon belief in separation and duality. Judgment is a frequency of separateness degenerative of the eternal Life Force. The need to judge is indicative of a greater need to love.

KINGDOM OF GOD: The eternal life consciousness of God, referred to often as the Kingdom of Heaven.

KING'S CHAMBER: Located in the pyramid at the center of the Holy Temple of God's house. At the pyramidal point in the King's Chamber, time stands still. The key opening the door to the chamber is love. If we come into the chamber with anything in our hand other than this key, we cannot remain. This is the "arc of the covenant." This is the beginning of the remembrance of eternal life.

LIFE FORCE: The energy propelling all forms to action. A regenerative energy like a miracle serum going into all of the life cells on every level, from the physical, to the mental, to the emotional, to the cellular of the earth itself.

LIGHT:

A Divine emanation, as opposed to physical light. Illumination of the Spirit. In itself a "living consciousness" controlled by Divine thought-forms.

LIGHT BEINGS:

Love frequency beings of high intensity who have left loneliness far behind only know union and communion with God. Sent to planet earth with the purpose and mission to guide, direct and assist in the lifting of consciousness.

LIQUID LIGHT:

Energy that moves with the rhythm of the infinite Merkabah carrying a frequency of intense vibration.

LOVE:

All there is, written in the cells of all life forms. Quickening agent in the Earth, the structure of the components of which is not known to human consciousness. As love is quickened in the structure of the human being, it will reveal the higher teachings of wisdom that come forth from the magnetic quality of this vibratory energy. Love is the frequency of light in which time stands still, and it is the magnetic force for co-creation keeping everything in balance. Love draws the darkness and absorbs it into itself. Love is the power uniting the universe and the spiritual glue keeping the children of God in eternal life. Love is the master key to all of the doors of the many mansions in God's house.

MANSION WORLDS: Myriad levels of soul emanation. Dimensions of consciousness or planes of existence.

MASTER KEY: Love.

MASTER TEACHER: Jesus.

MERCY: The gift of forgiving love within us only awaiting our acceptance.

MERKABAH: Spiritual, Divine light vehicle which protects and shields.

MESSIAH: Illuminated; enlightened by the Holy Spirit; endowed with a special mission. Visible manifestation in the earth of the Christ Principle. Not a person, but the light of God indwelling every man, woman and child.

MIND: God, the universal Principle. Three phases of: conscious mind, subconscious mind, and superconscious mind -- actually all states of consciousness in the one Universal Mind. Pure God thought.

MYSTICAL: Having spiritual meaning.

NEED: A call from the inner Self to release and to give that which we think we have need of. Give the need to God, and God will release from within the capacity to fill the need from within. The receiving of that which we thought we needed lies in the giving.

NEW AGE: The beginning of a paradigm shift in conscious perception to the true nature of reality. See Age of Ascension.

NEW BIRTH: Coming into a higher state of being fully conscious of our Divine and eternal nature. Birth into regenerative form of eternal life.

NEW CREATURE IN CHRIST: Birth of love in us, bringing forth the image and likeness of God.

NEW EARTH: Time of the Tree of Life manifesting, growing and giving of its fruit on the planet known as the good earth. Quickened by the seed of the presence and the power of eternal life; a bringing forth on earth of the image and likeness of the fruit that is innate within the seed. The new beginning.

NEW JERUSALEM: State of cosmic consciousness being anchored in the earth as referenced in Revelations. The next plane of conscious existence creating a universal pattern of wholeness. The New Creation.

NEW TEACHING: The Grace of the fathers is visited upon the children. The Grace of the mothers is visited upon the children. The Grace of God carries its seed into eternal life.

OM: Sound vibration of the soul. Mantric sound which is thought to be a complete expression of Brahman, used as a meditational guide to reach a state of inner peace. Sound code charging the body with the power of Divine Mind. Sacred syllable symbolizing the sum total of all energy and first cause. It means the "All."

OMEGA: The end.

OMNI ASHNI: Words from ancient manuscripts long forgotten which will help to unlock the doors of the inner chambers of the indwelling spiritual heart and move our awareness to deeper mansions of God's house. Meditated upon, these words will awaken the love vibration, of Jesus Christ and fulfill the mission written in our eternal heart.

OMNISCIENT: Having infinite awareness, knowledge and wisdom.

ONE PRESENCE &
ONE POWER: God.

OVERSOUL: Higher body of light exhibiting the perfect spiritual nature. Jesus Christ is the oversoul of this planet.

PEARL OF GREAT PRICE: Eternal wisdom and love. The one treasure beyond any price or value.

PEDUNCLE: Bud or beginning of a new phylum/life form in nature.

PLANET EARTH: Considered by Jesus Christ His incarnate home for which He is the oversoul. The earth is important in the fulfillment of the Divine Plan, birthing a peaceful state of consciousness which, added to the dimensions of consciousness already created in the universe, is a balancing factor necessary for the entire cosmos to function in Divine Order. The energy upon this planet is a particular graceful expression of God's drawingness into Itself. It is a place where possibilities can come into the fullness of expression. It is the planet of peace.

PRANAMED: Bowed position, heart above the head.

PRESTANCE: An elixir of love quickening the spiritual nature into the lower bodies. A code of remembrance of union captured in the cells of the entire human being and programmed to be activated at the time of the New Age now upon us. It is expressing itself in manifestation as the Divine Love of

God.

PROGRAMMING: The advancement of a project through instructions toward a solution.

PURE HEART: Free from anxiety, resentment, selfishness, guilt, jealousy, and other error states of mind. A state of pure consciousness acquired through surrender.

PYRAMIDAL POINT: Initiation center to higher dimensional consciousness located within. Key vortex point.

RACE CONSCIOUSNESS: Totality of beliefs, thoughts, memories, feelings, and experiences of the collective race mind.

REGENERATION: Spiritual renewal into bodies of light. Unification of Spirit, soul, and body in spiritual oneness.

REMEMBRANCE OF UNION: Restoration of Divine Memory empowering us to become conscious co-creators with God.

RESURRECTION: Complete transformation of body into Divine Order as every cell becomes immortal. This takes place as the elixir of love is quickened in the soul through forgiveness of the patterns of remembrance that have not been in alignment with the perfection written in the heart. A body spiritually free in the fullness of the Holy Spirit.

RIVER OF LIFE: Peace flowing at the center of our being coming from and returning to the Source. Through the activity of prayer, meditation and devotion, we are drawn into the river of life in the chamber of the heart lifting us up into a new creature in Christ Jesus.

SELF: Christ within. The Christ Self is the birth of the Life Force taking us into God's house and bringing us back into the arms of love.

SHEKINAH: The everlasting I AM Presence of God. Sanctification of the molecular form of the inner universe by the feminine nature of God expressing as the Holy Spirit.

SON: Created in the image and likeness of God. God's idea of humankind in expression.

SOURCE:

God.

SPIRITUAL NAME:

The name written within our heart as the individualization of the Messiah within us, known only to our I AM Presence.

STAR CHILD:

Being of Light -- each one of us.

STAR OF DAVID:

A precious symbol being placed in the hearts of the awareness of humankind. The symbol of the ascending mind of the human being and the descending consciousness of the spiritual human being, merging and bringing into union the two which are one.

STILL SMALL VOICE:

The voice of Spirit or the higher Self within.

SURRENDER:

Let go and let God. The way of entrance into the Kingdom of God. Being "out of control." Trust at the highest level.

THANKSGIVING:

Grateful thoughts. A vibratory energy of great power which is a magnetic attractive force for Grace. Causative energy of acceptance.

TIME-SPACE CONTINUUM: A four dimensional continuum consisting of three spatial coordinates (height, width and depth) and one temporal coordinate (time).

TREE OF KNOWLEDGE OF
GOOD & EVIL: Discerning capacity of the mind. Symbolic of discernment through the comparison of opposites. Necessary wisdom in becoming conscious co-creators.

TREE OF LIFE: Symbolic of the absolute life principle established by Divine Mind. The consciousness of eternal life in the body is its fruit.

TRIBULATION: Automatic feature of our universe that serves as a "wake up call." Path of suffering and trial -- the way of darkness. The effect of a consciousness centered in the sense of separation.

TWIN FLAME OF SOUL: The eternal flame of the inner Christ drawing us into a mystical marriage or union in consciousness with our true Self. It is that aspect of Soul which has yearned to find itself remembered through aeons of incarnation in co-creation.

TWO BY TWO:　The measure of One. How we shall enter God's house. The coming together of two creates an energy pattern of Oneness that explodes the possibility of fulfillment. If two of us in the earth come together agreeing in relationship for birthing of the truth, it shall be accomplished in His name.

UNION:　Universal oneness of God, humankind, the universe and all creation. Christ Consciousness.

VIBRATIONAL FREQUENCY:　The rate of vibration or motion within a particular field of energy.

VORTEX:　Whirling, circular vacuum. Irresistible force drawing into its current all that surrounds it. Rapid rotatory movement of cosmic matter about a center.

WORD:　The immaculate conception in God Mind of the principle of Christ made flesh. The divine dynamic, self-revelation of God. Indwelling of "Sonship."

WINGS OF SPIRIT FOUNDATION
CATALOG

The Return of the Dove
Diadra
Item # 0001   Softbound Book $12.95
Item # T001   Audio Tapes (3 tape set) $15.95

The Dove is the symbol of the Holy Spirit
which is sweeping the consciousness of
humanity in a purification process. Diadra
Presents the following concepts:
  We Are Not Alone
  The Tree of Life
  Meditation with Omni Ashni
  Prestance, the Elixir of Love
  Beyond the Reasoning Mind
  It is Written in Your Heart
  Empowerment to Ascension

Holy Spirit Regeneration
Diadra
Item # T002 Audio Tapes (4 tape set) $19.95

This live recording of Diadra's workshop
explores the depth of the purification
process and helps each child of God
understand the individual soul's journey
in the Divine Plan. Among the topics
addressed are:
  Holy Spirit Regeneration
  The Soul's Journey
  Mystical Prayer Techniques
  The Role of Jesus Christ in Regeneration
  Death and Eternal Life

The Five Step Prayer Method
Diadra
Item # T003 (one tape) $7.95

Side one teaches and inspires with simple
thoughts on meditation that cover the
5-step prayer process and experiences
encountered in the silence. Side two
features Diadra guiding a gentle meditation
accompanied by relaxing music that helps the
listener reach deep levels if inner peace and communion.

ORDER FORM

To Order any Book or Tape:
· Write the title and Item # below
· Make checks payable to Wings of Spirit Foundation
· Payment by check/money order must be in U.S. funds only
· Texas residents please add 8.25% sales tax
· Shipping rates as follows within USA only

Price	UPS	Mail
Up to $15	$4.50	$3.25
$15.01 - $50.00	$5.75	$4.75
$50.01 - $80.00	$6.75	$5.75
$80.01 - $99.00	$8.00	$6.75

Allow 5 - 8 days for UPS and 3 - 4 weeks for 4th class mail
Prices are subject to change

Mail orders to Wings of Spirit Foundation · 6757 Arapaho · Suite 711 · Box 345 · Dallas, TX 75248

Item #	Qty.	Description	Price	Amount
			Subtotal	
		Sales Tax: (TX 8.25%)		
		Shipping and Handling (each address)		
		Total		

Ship To: (Please use street address if UPS delivery is selected)

Name: _____

Address: _____

City: _____ State: _____ Zip: _____

☐ Please add this name to the *Wings of Spirit* mailing list

Wings of Spirit Foundation is a not-for-profit organization that is supported solely through the tithes, love offerings and contributions of you, the people, who believe in the Will of God impulsing global transformation and world peace. Your gifts are literally brought to the ALTAR OF PRAYER and dedicated to the vision. Through the activity of grace they are returned to you one hundred fold.

Wings of Spirit Foundation
(214) 233-2992

WINGS OF SPIRIT FOUNDATION

As part of its global vision, Wings of Spirit Foundation has launched the **"String of Pearls"** prayer circle concept involving small groups of individuals of all faiths gathering together in homes, churches, workplaces, etc., for the sole, simple purpose of intending the mind and heart toward the Will of God. When a sufficient number of prayer circles are formed in each city, Wings of Spirit Foundation will be sponsoring local "Gathering of Light" event concerts of worship and praise with 1000 member choirs, dance, inspirational music, special effects and more. Starting in Dallas, Texas, Wings of Spirit will be taking this vision to every major city in the USA and globally. For more information, or to become an active part of the vision, contact:

Wings of Spirit
P.O. Box 285
Blowing Rock, N.C. 28605

Ph: (828) 265-4017   Fax: (828) 263-0101
E-mail: wings@wingsofspirit.com Website: wings-of-spirit.org/